# The Essentials
## *of*
# Buddhist Meditation

The publication of this book has been enabled by
a generous donation from Upāsaka Guo Ke.

**A Note on the Proper Care of Dharma Materials**

Traditional Buddhist cultures treat books on Dharma as sacred. Hence it
is considered disrespectful to place them in a low position, to read them
when lying down, or to place them where they might be damaged by food
or drink.

# THE ESSENTIALS
## *of*
# BUDDHIST MEDITATION

A Classic *Śamatha-Vipaśyanā* Meditation Manual:

## *The Essentials for Practicing Calming-and-Insight & Dhyāna Meditation*
### 修習止觀坐禪法要

By the Great Tiantai Meditation Master & Exegete:
Śramaṇa Zhiyi (Chih-i)
(538–597 CE)

Translation by Bhikshu Dharmamitra

KALAVINKA PRESS
Seattle, Washington
WWW.KALAVINKAPRESS.ORG

**KALAVINKA PRESS**
8603 39th Ave SW
Seattle, WA 98136 USA

**WWW.KALAVINKAPRESS.ORG / WWW.KALAVINKA.ORG**

Kalavinka Press is the publishing arm of the Kalavinka Dharma Association, a non-profit organized exclusively for religious educational purposes as allowed within the meaning of section 501(c)3 of the Internal Revenue Code. KDA was founded in 1990 and gained formal approval in 2004 by the United States Internal Revenue Service as a 501(c)3 non-profit organization to which donations are tax deductible.

Donations to KDA are accepted by mail and on the Kalavinka website where numerous free Dharma translations and excerpts from Kalavinka publications are available in digital format.

**PUBLISHER'S CATALOGING-IN-PUBLICATION DATA**

Zhiyi (Chih-i), 538–597.

[Xiuxi zhiguan zuo chan fa yao. English translation.]
The Essentials of Buddhist Meditation. The Essentials for Practicing Calming-and-Insight and Dhyāna Meditation.

Translated by Bhikshu Dharmamitra. – 1st ed. – Seattle, WA: Kalavinka Press, 2009.

p. ; cm.
ISBN: 978-1-935413-00-4
Includes: Song-dynasty Yuanzhao preface; text outline; facing-page Chinese source text in both traditional and simplified scripts; notes.
Other author: Yuanzhao (Yüan chao), 1048–1116.

1. Tiantai Buddhism – Doctrines – Early works to 1800. 2. Meditation – Tiantai Buddhism – Early works to 1800. 3. Śamatha (Buddhism) – Early works to 1800. 4. Vipaśyanā (Buddhism) – Early works to 1800. I. Yuanzhao. II. Title.

2009920868
0902

Cover and interior designed and composed by Bhikshu Dharmamitra

Dedicated to the memory of the selfless and marvelous life of the
Venerable Dhyāna Master Hsuan Hua, the Weiyang Ch'an Patriarch
and the very personification of the Bodhisattva Path.

**DHYĀNA MASTER HSUAN HUA**

宣化禪師

**1918–1995**

## ACKNOWLEDGMENTS

The accuracy and readability of of these first ten books of translations have been significantly improved with the aid of extensive corrections, preview comments, and editorial suggestions generously contributed by Bhikkhu Bodhi, Jon Babcock, Timothy J. Lenz, Upasaka Feng Ling, Upāsaka Guo Ke, Upāsikā Min Li, and Richard Robinson. Additional valuable editorial suggestions and corrections were offered by Bhikshu Huifeng and Bruce Munson.

The publication of the initial set of ten translation volumes has been assisted by substantial donations to the Kalavinka Dharma Association by Bill and Peggy Brevoort, Freda Chen, David Fox, Upāsaka Guo Ke, Chenping and Luther Liu, Sunny Lou, Jimi Neal, and "Leo L." (*Camellia sinensis folium*). Additional donations were offered by Doug Adams, Diane Hodgman, Bhikshu Huifeng, Joel and Amy Lupro, Richard Robinson, Ching Smith, and Sally and Ian Timm.

Were it not for the ongoing material support provided by my late guru's Dharma Realm Buddhist Association and the serene translation studio provided by Seattle's Bodhi Dhamma Center, creation of this translation would have been immensely more difficult.

Most importantly, it would have been impossible for me to produce this translation without the Dharma teachings provided by my late guru, the Weiyang Ch'an Patriarch, Dharma teacher, and exegete, the Venerable Master Hsuan Hua.

## CITATION AND ROMANIZATION PROTOCOLS

Kalavinka Press *Taisho* citation style adds text numbers after volume numbers and before page numbers to assist rapid CBETA digital searches.

Romanization, where used, is Pinyin with the exception of names and terms already well-recognized in Wade-Giles.

## THE CHINESE TEXT

This translation is supplemented by inclusion of Chinese source text on verso pages in both traditional and simplified scripts. Taisho-supplied variant readings from other editions are presented as Chinese endnotes.

This Chinese text and its variant readings are from the April, 2004 version of the Chinese Buddhist Electronic Text Association's digital edition of the Taisho compilation of the Buddhist canon.

Those following the translation in the Chinese should be aware that Taisho scripture punctuation is not traceable to original editions, is often erroneous and misleading, and is probably best ignored altogether. (In any case, accurate reading of Classical Chinese does not require any punctuation at all.)

# GENERAL TABLE OF CONTENTS

# DIRECTORY TO CHAPTER SUBSECTIONS

## Master Zhiyi's Preface

## Chapter 1: Fulfillment of the Prerequisite Conditions   39

## Chapter 4:  Making Adjustments                                  77

## Chapter 10: Realization of the Fruits     189

# Introduction

## The Nature and Present Import of This Text

Due to its clarity and comprehensiveness in describing the crucially important factors involved in understanding and practicing Buddhist meditation, this present work, *The Essentials for Practicing Calming-and-Insight and Dhyāna Meditation,* is one of the most important introductory meditation manuals ever authored in the two millennia-long course of Sino-Buddhist history.

These very same qualities of clarity and comprehensiveness make this text by Master Zhiyi (Chih-i) a genuinely useful and reliable meditation-instruction resource for English-speaking students of the Buddha's Dharma. Although relatively short, *The Essentials* includes in condensed form the entire scope of teachings necessary for practicing what is right and avoiding what is wrong as one pursues the practice of Buddhist meditation. As such, it offers both the beginning student and the long-term Dharma practitioner immediate access to the essentials required for learning, enhancing, or rectifying Buddhist meditation practice.

This is equally true for traditions of practice not as readily identifiable with "calming-and-insight" training, as for example Ch'an meditation. Indeed, it is hard to envision how a practitioner of Ch'an meditation could make very meaningful progress in that radical and sudden approach to meditation without having first developed a solid understanding and practice of most of what is taught in Master Zhiyi's *Essentials of Buddhist Meditation.*

## The Author and His Works on Meditation

The author of this text is the famous meditation master and exegete, Śramaṇa Zhiyi (538–597 CE), one of the most brilliant and widely-respected figures in the history of Chinese Buddhism, a monastic eminence well-known for textual exegesis on numerous works, for brilliance in refining and broadening the Tiantai teaching school's hermeneutic presentation, and for authoring Chinese Buddhism's four most important meditation texts explaining right practice of the calming-and-insight meditation discipline standard in Indian Buddhism. Specifically, those works are:

1. *The Great Calming-and-Insight* (摩訶止觀 / T46.1911.001–140)
2. *An Explanation of the Dharma Gateway of Dhyāna Pāramitā* (釋禪波羅蜜次第法門 / T46.1916.475–548)
3. *The Essentials for Practicing Calming-and-Insight and Dhyāna Meditation* (修習止觀坐禪法要 / T46.1915.462–475)
4. *The Six Gates to the Sublime* (六妙法門 / T46.1917.549–555)

Of the above four texts, this translation is the third. (I have also translated the fourth and am publishing it under separate cover.)

### The Circumstances Occasioning the Writing of this Text

The immediate personal cause for the writing of this text was Master Zhiyi's desire to produce a simple but comprehensive meditation text to help his brother break through life-threatening karmic obstacles.

The larger cause for writing this text was the wish to introduce a short and easily understood foundational meditation manual clarifying right meditation practice for wider use among Buddhist practitioners. This was done at a time still early in the history of Buddhism in China when right meditation practice was not always well understood by students of Dharma and when instruction in meditation was not universally available. Although deep understanding of meditation practice was probably quite common among the learned monastic elites, short, clear, and comprehensive texts addressing the needs of the larger Buddhist community were rare.

### Primary Doctrinal Focus of this Text

The terms I render in the title and throughout the text as "calming-and-insight" are the standard Buddhist technical terms describing the primary aspects of traditional Indian Buddhist meditation (Sanskrit: *śamatha-vipaśyanā*; Pali: *samatha-vipassanā*). Modern Tibetan-tradition translations commonly render these primary meditation practice elements with such terms as "calm abiding and special insight" (*zhi gnas, lhag mthong*). Southern-tradition translations commonly refer to the former as "calming meditation" or "*samatha* meditation" (often linking it to breath-focused meditation or *ānāpāna*), while identifying the latter as "insight," "insight meditation," or "vipassana meditation."

Given this common ground as a point of reference, we may realize that this short work provides training in the bases for correct understanding and practice of the most standard form of meditation common to all Buddhist traditions. This work is in no way a text devoted to uniquely Sino-Buddhist forms of meditation. The roots of all teachings presented in *Essentials* are standard in classic Indian Buddhism. Although it would be easy enough to demonstrate how calming-and-contemplation meditation is fundamentally no different from Bodhidharma's Ch'an meditation (Sanskrit: *dhyāna*; Korean: *son*; Japanese: *zen*), this work not only does not teach "Ch'an" *per se*, it does not even mention it.

### The Structure of the Text

I have included the preface written by the Song dynasty monk, Yuanzhao, half a millennium after Master Zhiyi passed on because it so well describes the text's content and significance.

The *Essentials* text proper begins with a brief prefatory discussion by Master Zhiyi himself in which he emphasizes the importance of balanced calming-and-insight practice which does not favor the stillness of "calming" over the development of wisdom realizations through analytic "insight" and does not favor "insight" over "calming." He compares the two primary elements of meditation practice to the two wheels of a cart or the two wings of a bird, two cases wherein "imbalance" is clearly untenable.

Master Zhiyi then segues into the text proper by listing the ten chapter titles. The chapters are arranged in a practical sequence proceeding from preliminaries to actual practice to important related topics. I now provide a brief content synopsis for each chapter:

**Chapter One:** "Fulfillment of Prerequisite Conditions." The concerns here are the prerequisite needs of: moral virtue and purification of bad karma; adequacy of clothing, food, and domicile; withdrawal from involvements; and proximity to spiritual guidance from a genuinely reliable source.

**Chapter Two:** "Renunciation of Desires." The topic here is facilitating focused meditation practice by withdrawal from the distractions inherent in attachment to sense-object data comprised by visual forms, sounds, smells, tastes, and touchables.

**Chapter Three:** "Elimination of the Hindrances." The five hindrances discussed are: desire in the mind for the aforementioned sense objects; ill-will; "lethargy-and-sleepiness"; "excitedness-and-regretfulness"; and afflicted doubt in self, guru, or Dharma.

**Chapter Four:** "Making Adjustments." The primary topics here are: a) the necessary adjustments to food and sleep when not actually seated in meditation; and b) the appropriate adjustments in body, breath, and mind when entering meditation, abiding in meditation, and emerging from meditation.

**Chapter Five:** "Implementation of Skillful Means." This is a very brief discussion of five essential factors as they apply to the practice of meditation, namely: zeal, vigor, mindfulness, wise discernment, and single-mindedness.

**Chapter Six:** "The Actual Cultivation." This very detailed chapter goes directly into the practice of calming-and-insight, giving particular focus to: countering mental coarseness and scatteredness; countering "sinking" and "floating" mind states; applying either calming or insight as best suited to exigent circumstances; countering "subtle" mind states conducing to attachment; and using calming-and-insight to achieve balance between meditative absorption and wisdom. Instruction is provided regarding the use of calming-and-contemplation at the gates of each of the sense gates of eye, ear, nose, tongue, body, and intellectual mind and also while sitting, standing, walking, lying down, talking, and doing things.

**Chapter Seven:** "Manifestation of Roots of Goodness." This chapter primarily covers mind states arising in meditation as effects from specific types of prior spiritual cultivation, in particular: cultivation of the internal energetics of meditation; contemplation of impurity; cultivation of kindness; contemplation of causality, cultivation of mindfulness of the Buddha. It then deals with the issue of distinguishing between signs of false meditative absorptions and signs of genuine meditative absorptions. The chapter concludes with an exhortation to pursue the establishment of yet more good karmic causes productive of auspicious future karmic effects.

**Chapter Eight:** "Recognition of the Work of Demons." This chapter deals with a topic little discussed in Western Buddhist circles, that of "demons," phenomena dismissed by many as ancient superstition. Here, the various categories of problematic ghosts, spirits, and demon-generated afflictions are catalogued along with the means of driving them away through calming, through insight, through rectification of mind, through mantras, through repentances, through precept recitation, through uncompromising ongoing karmic correctness, and through assistance of the guru.

**Chapter Nine:** "Treatment of Disorders." This chapter deals with traditional means of countering physical and mental disturbances arising through karmic obstacles or unskillful meditation practice.

**Chapter Ten:** "Realization of the Fruits." The concerns here are in distinguishing between provisional and ultimate contemplations while also describing the nature of the high-level, later-stage meditation practice of those well advanced on the path to buddhahood. The discussion concludes with a clear statement of essential prerequisites for success in meditation practice.

### Special Aspects of This Text

In reflecting on the matter, I have noticed that this particular work by Master Zhiyi possesses a number of important special aspects making it unique among Buddhist meditation texts so far available in English translation, among which are the following:

First, unlike most works dealing with calming-and-insight, even though its teachings are for the most part independent of any particular tradition, the doctrinal framing of this text is distinctly mahāyānistic. By this, I mean to say that the tenor of its discussions more-or-less assume that all practice is carried out in the context of the altruistic path devoted to universal spiritual liberation.

Concrete manifestations of this "mahāyānistic orientation" are found in a few of the teachings found in *The Essentials*. For instance: a) In the chapter on the prerequisites as it relates to purification of negative karma through repentances; b) In the chapter on dealing with demons, specifically in the recommendation of mantras as means to counter negative influences; and c) In the chapter on realization of the fruits of practice, specifically as regards distinguishing what is and is not an "ultimate" contemplation.

Second, this text also seems to be unique among meditation texts found in English translation in the unusual comprehensiveness of the topics it covers. That is to say, it does not simply describe the details of how to meditate. Rather it deals with everything of genuine importance related to the practice of meditation. Examples of these crucial related issues include specific instructions on:

1. Fulfilling crucial prerequisite conditions which are essential to entering deep meditation states.
2. Eliminating the five hindrances blocking all meaningful progress in cultivating meditation.
3. Making essential adjustments to food, sleep, body, breath, and mind.

4. Dealing with unbalanced development of calming (*śamatha*) versus insight (*vipaśyanā*) so as to ensure acquisition of not just meditative absorption, but also genuine wisdom.

5. Countering "floating" mind states and "sinking" mind states blocking entry into meditative absorption.

6. Distinguishing between false and deceptive meditation states leading away from the Path and genuinely beneficial meditation states serving progress on the Path.

7. Countering various types of meditation sickness and negative spiritual influences commonly encountered in the cultivation of meditative absorption.

Third, *The Essentials* may also be unique in describing "insight" (*vipaśyanā*) at the highest level of realization of emptiness of all encountered phenomena at each of the six sense gates and in all circumstances, whether walking, sitting, standing, lying down, doing things, or talking, while describing "calming" (*śamatha*) at the highest level of realization wherein cognition of reality silences discursive thought and enforces deep wakeful serenity.

As a side note, reflection on the above-mentioned definitions of "calming" and "insight" makes the rationale behind classic Chinese "Ch'an" practice much easier to grasp for those heretofore inured to more classic dogmas of what is and is not calming-and-insight meditation. In short, reflecting on this, one realizes that Ch'an practice is a radically direct methodology for achieving the very same aims of calming-and-contemplation and is no different from calming-and-insight practice. When correctly understood and practiced, Bodhidharma's Ch'an meditation precipitates and enforces both complete "calming" and complete "insight."

Having first studied the present text, the identity of Ch'an practice with the other more widely recognized traditions of Indian Buddhist meditation becomes yet more obvious when one proceeds next to study Master Zhiyi's other short meditation text, *The Six Gates to the Sublime* which is also devoted to explaining a classic approach of early Indian Buddhist meditation practice.

### Stylistic Factors Affecting this Translation

Although I don't doubt there is room to improve the smoothness of this translation even while retaining precise accuracy, there nonetheless are some stylistic limitations and circumlocutional prolixity imposed by my default insistence on strictly literal translation. Also, the translation style may seem archaic or formal. This is for the most part because the Chinese text itself is written in a somewhat archaic and formal style.

Although many outline headings originate with Master Baojing's outline of the text, most of the numerous and detailed outline headings found in the English translation originate with the translator. (These are enclosed in brackets.) I inserted these additional headings because I feel that complex texts are made much more accessible to the English reader through introduction of more detailed outlining. I do not pretend my structural analysis of the text is infallible. There is probably room for improvement in the outline as presented in "Directory to Chapter Subsections" and as interwoven with the translated text.

### In Summation

I first produced a preliminary draft of this translation in 1992 and, owing to the importance of the work, I have allowed various copyrighted provisional drafts to be posted on the Kalavinka internet websites since then. Because the present version of the translation is immensely improved in accuracy over previous versions, it should in all cases be preferred as the definitive edition. It gives me great pleasure to be able to introduce such a potentially beneficial meditation text into the world of Western Buddhism, not least because confusion about right meditation practice is still so very widespread.

I would like to express particular gratitude to those who have reviewed the Chinese and English of the text, pointing out problems in earlier drafts of this work.

Due to the terseness of the language and the abstruseness of the concepts and practices treated, it is likely that there will be room for further refinement of aspects of this translation. I hope that specialists or practitioners encountering errors or infelicities will favor me with recommendations for improvement, forwarding such suggestions via the Kalavinka websites.

I especially hope that Buddhist practitioners may find this text useful in development of meditation practice and in advancement on the Path.

Bhikshu Dharmamitra
Seattle, New Year's Day, 2008

# THE ESSENTIALS
## *of*
# BUDDHIST MEDITATION

Tiantai Master Zhiyi's Classic Meditation Manual:

## *The Essentials for Practicing*
## *Calming-and-Insight & Dhyāna Meditation*

English Translation by Bhikshu Dharmamitra

[0462a06]　　　[1]天台止观有四本。一曰圆顿止观。大师于荆州玉泉寺说。章安记为十卷。二曰渐次止观。在瓦官寺说。弟子法慎记。本三十卷。章安治定为十卷。今禅波罗蜜是。三曰不定止观。即陈尚书令毛喜请大师出。有一卷。今六妙门是。四曰小止观。即今文是。大师为俗兄陈针出。寔大部之梗概。入道之枢机。曰止观。曰定慧。曰寂照。曰明静。皆同出而异名也。若夫穷万法之源底。考诸佛之修证。莫若止观。天台大师灵山亲承。承止观也。大苏妙悟。悟止观也。三昧所修。修止观也。纵辩而说。说止观也。故曰。说己心中所行法门。则知台教宗部虽繁。

[0462a06]　　　[1]天台止觀有四本。一曰圓頓止觀。大師於荊州玉泉寺說。章安記為十卷。二曰漸次止觀。在瓦官寺說。弟子法慎記。本三十卷。章安治定為十卷。今禪波羅蜜是。三曰不定止觀。即陳尚書令毛喜請大師出。有一卷。今六妙門是。四曰小止觀。即今文是。大師為俗兄陳鍼出。寔大部之梗概。入道之樞機。曰止觀。曰定慧。曰寂照。曰明靜。皆同出而異名也。若夫窮萬法之源底。考諸佛之修證。莫若止觀。天台大師靈山親承。承止觀也。大蘇妙悟。悟止觀也。三昧所修。修止觀也。縱辯而說。說止觀也。故曰。說己心中所行法門。則知台教宗部雖繁。

简体字　　　　　正體字

# THE YUANZHAO PREFACE

**By the Song Dynasty Monk, Yuanzhao (釋元照: 1048–1116 CE)**

There are four calming-and-insight texts in the Tiantai tradition: The first, known as the "perfect and sudden," was presented in the form of lectures by the Great Master at Yuquan ("Jade Spring") Monastery in Jingzhou Prefecture. Zhang'an (章安) transcribed it in ten fascicles.

The second, known as the "gradual and sequential," was lectured at Waguan ("Tiled House") Monastery. Disciple Fashen (法慎) transcribed it. Originally comprising thirty fascicles, Zhang'an edited it into ten fascicles. It is what is known today as the *Dhyāna Pāramitā*.

The third, known as the "unfixed," is the one which the Chen Dynasty Chief State Secretary (尚書令), Maoxi (毛喜), requested the Great Master to issue. It consists of a single fascicle known today as the *Six Gates to the Sublime*.

The fourth, known as the *Smaller Calming-and-Insight*, is this very text. The Great Master brought it forth for his elder brother, Chenzhen. Truly, this is a condensation of the large edition and a presentation of the very crux of the means for entering the Path.

As for what is described as "calming-and-insight," or as "meditative absorption and wisdom," or as "quiescence and illumination," or as "luminous clarity and stillness"—these are all instances of different designations describing the very same concepts.

Now, as for what reaches to the very bottom of the myriad dharmas' source and permits one to directly verify the cultivation and realization of the Buddhas, none compare to calming-and-insight. And as for what the Great Master of the Tiantai tradition personally received at Mount Gṛdhrakūṭa—he received calming-and-insight. As for the marvelous awakening of the great arousing, it is the awakening to calming-and-insight. As for what is cultivated in samādhi, it is calming-and-insight. As for what is described when eloquence is allowed to flourish, it is calming-and-insight.

Therefore, one may say that, when it comes to explicating those Dharma gateways of one's own mind which are practiced, although the texts of the Tiantai teaching tradition are elaborate and numerous,

要归不出止观。舍止观不足以明天台道。不足以议天台教。故入道者不可不学。学者不可不修。奈何叔世寡薄驰走声利。或胶固于名相。或混肴于暗证。其书虽存。而止观之道蔑闻于世。得不为之痛心疾首哉。今以此书命工镂板。将使闻者见者。皆植大乘缘种。况有修有证者。则其利尚可量耶。予因对校乃为叙云。时绍圣二年仲秋朔。馀杭郡释元照序

要歸不出止觀。舍止觀不足以明天台道。不足以議天台教。故入道者不可不學。學者不可不修。奈何叔世寡薄馳走聲利。或膠固於名相。或混肴於闇證。其書雖存。而止觀之道蔑聞於世。得不為之痛心疾首哉。今以此書命工鏤板。將使聞者見者。皆植大乘緣種。況有修有證者。則其利尚可量耶。予因對校乃為敘云。時紹聖二年仲秋朔。餘杭郡釋元照序

簡体字

正體字

one should realize that the essentials to which they return do not go beyond calming-and-insight.

Were one to stray from calming-and-insight, one's abilities would be inadequate to clearly understand the Path as described in the Tiantai tradition and would be inadequate to even discuss the meaning of the Tiantai tradition's teachings. Therefore, one who would enter the Path simply cannot fail to study [calming-and-insight]. One who would study it cannot fail to cultivate it. How then could one, like the shallow learners of a decadent age, merely chase after reputation and profit, course in rigid attachments to mere designations, or indulge muddled relishing of only the dimmest sorts of meditative realizations?

Although the texts devoted to it remain extant, still, the path of calming-and-insight is but little heard of in the World these days. On realizing this, is it even possible to not experience an aching heart and pain-filled mind?

I write this preface now on the occasion of commissioning the carving of new woodblocks for the printing of this text. May this event cause all who hear it explained or lay eyes on it to plant the seeds of causal affinity with the Great Vehicle. How much the more so might this be the case where there are those who cultivate according to it or gain realizations based on it? Were this to occur, could the benefits issuing from it even be measurable?

Since I had to proofread this work [prior to releasing it for printing], I took that as an occasion to write this preface.

Preface by the Shakyan monk, Yuanzhao.

Composed in Yuhang Prefecture, in the second year of the Shaosheng reign period (1096 CE), on the first day of autumn's second lunar month.

| 简体字 | 正體字 |
|---|---|
| 修习止观坐禅法要（一曰童蒙止观亦名小止观） | 修習止觀坐禪法要（一曰童蒙止觀亦名小止觀） |
| 天台山修禅寺沙门智顗述 | 天台山修禪寺沙門智顗述 |
| [0462b05] [2]诸恶莫作。众善奉行。自净其意。是诸佛教 | [0462b05] [2]諸惡莫作。眾善奉行。自淨其意。是諸佛教 |
| [0462b07] 若夫泥洹之法。入乃多途论其急要。不出止观二法。所以然者。止乃伏结之初门。观是断惑之正要。止则爱养心识之善资。观则策发神解之妙术。止是禅定之胜因。观是智慧之由藉。若人成就定慧二法。斯乃自利利人法皆具足。故法华经云。佛自住大乘如其所得法定慧力庄严以此度众生。 | [0462b07] 若夫泥洹之法。入乃多途論其急要。不出止觀二法。所以然者。止乃伏結之初門。觀是斷惑之正要。止則愛養心識之善資。觀則策發神解之妙術。止是禪定之勝因。觀是智慧之由藉。若人成就定慧二法。斯乃自利利人法皆具足。故法華經云。佛自住大乘如其所得法定慧力莊嚴以此度眾生。 |

# Tiantai Master Zhiyi's Preface

I. Introductory Section

  A. Citing a Quatrain to Indicate the Grand Design

To refrain from doing any manner of evil,
To respectfully perform all varieties of good,
To carry out the purification of one's own mind—
It is this which constitutes the teaching of all Buddhas.[1]

  B. Introduction Proper: Conditions Occasioning Creation of This Text

    1. Brief Indication of the Essential Nature of Calming and Insight

As for the dharma of nirvāṇa, there are many paths of entry into it. However, if we discuss those which are crucially essential, they do not go beyond the two dharmas of calming and insight.

    2. Commendation of the Marvelous Functions of Calming and Insight

How is this so? Calming (śamatha) constitutes the initial method through which one is able to suppress the fetters (saṃyojana).[2] Insight (vipaśyanā) is the primary essential through which one is able to cut off the delusions. Calming then is the wholesome provision with which one kindly nurtures the mind and consciousness. Insight then is the marvelous technique which stimulates the development of spiritual understanding. Calming is the supreme cause for the manifestation of dhyāna absorption. Insight is the origin of wisdom.

    3. Clarification of the Supreme Benefits of Calming and Insight

      a. Clarification Proper

If a person perfects the two dharmas of meditative absorption and wisdom, then this amounts to the complete fulfillment of the dharma of benefiting both oneself and others.

      b. Scriptural Citation

Hence the *Dharma Blossom Sutra* states, "The Buddha himself abides in the Great Vehicle. Such dharmas as he has realized are adorned by the power of meditative absorption and wisdom. He employs these in delivering beings to liberation."[2]

当知此之二法如车之双轮
鸟之两翼。若偏修习即堕
邪倒。故经云。若偏修禅
定福德。不学智慧。名之
曰愚。偏学知慧不修禅定
福德名之曰狂。狂愚之过
虽小不同。邪见轮转盖无
差别。若不均等此则行乖
圆备。何能疾登极果。故
经云。声闻之人定力多故
不见佛性。十住菩萨智慧
力多。虽见佛性而不明
了。诸佛如来定慧力等。
是故了了见于佛性。以此
推之。止观岂非泥洹大果
之要门。行人修行之胜
路。众德圆满之指归。无
上极果之正体也。若如是
知者止观法门实非浅。故
欲接引始学之流辈。开蒙
冥

简体字

當知此之二法如車之雙輪
鳥之兩翼。若偏修習即墮
邪倒。故經云。若偏修禪
定福德。不學智慧。名之
曰愚。偏學知慧不修禪定
福德名之曰狂。狂愚之過
雖小不同。邪見輪轉蓋無
差別。若不均等此則行乖
圓備。何能疾登極果。故
經云。聲聞之人定力多故
不見佛性。十住菩薩智慧
力多。雖見佛性而不明
了。諸佛如來定慧力等。
是故了了見於佛性。以此
推之。止觀豈非泥洹大果
之要門。行人修行之勝
路。眾德圓滿之指歸。無
上極果之正體也。若如是
知者止觀法門實非淺。故
欲接引始學之流輩。開曚
冥

正體字

4. UNDESIRABLE ASPECTS OF INEQUALITY IN CALMING AND INSIGHT

a. EXPLANATION PROPER

One should realize that these two dharmas are like the two wheels of a cart or like the two wings of a bird. If the cultivation of them becomes one-sided, one immediately falls into error-ridden inverted views.

b. SCRIPTURAL CITATION

Hence a sutra states, "If a person is one-sided in the cultivation of dhyāna absorption and merit and thus neglects the study of wisdom, this results in delusion. If one indulges in the one-sided study of wisdom and thus neglects the cultivation of dhyāna absorption and its meritorious qualities, this results in derangement."[4]

Although there are some minor differences in the faults associated with delusion and derangement, still, the erroneous views developing from the two conditions are generally no different. If one fails to maintain even balance in this, then one's practice deviates from what would be perfect. How then could one achieve a swift ascent to the most ultimate result?

5. THE NECESSITY OF EVENLY BALANCED CALMING AND INSIGHT

a. SCRIPTURAL CITATION ILLUSTRATING IMPORTANCE

Hence a sutra declares, "Because the Śrāvaka disciples are more developed in their powers of meditative absorption, they are unable to perceive the buddha nature. The bodhisattvas abiding on the ten grounds (bhūmi) are more developed in the power of wisdom. Although they do perceive the buddha nature, still, that perception has not developed into complete clarity. The powers of meditative absorption and wisdom are equally developed in the Buddhas, the Tathāgatas. Consequently, they possess absolute understanding and perception of the buddha nature."[5]

Extrapolating from this, how could calming-and-insight not constitute the essential entryway into the great result of nirvāṇa, the supreme path for the cultivation of the practitioner, the common point of confluence for perfect fulfillment of the manifold virtues, and the very substance of the unsurpassed and ultimate result?

b. CLARIFYING THE RATIONALE IN THIS EXPLANATION OF CALMING-AND-INSIGHT

If one understands accordingly, then one will understand that this Dharma entryway of calming-and-insight is truly not a shallow one. When one wishes to draw in and lead along those who have only just begun to study—when one wishes to instruct the untutored

而进道。说易行难。岂可广论深妙。今略明十意。以示初心行人登正道之阶梯。入泥洹之等级。寻者当愧为行之难成。毋鄙斯文之浅近也。若心称言旨于一晌间。则智断难量神解莫测。若虚搆文言情乖所说。空延岁月取证无由。事等贫人数他财宝。于己何益者哉

[0462c03]　　具缘第一　诃欲第二　弃盖第三　调和第四　方便第五　正修第六　善发第七　觉魔第八治病第九　证果第十

而進道。說易行難。豈可廣論深妙。今略明十意。以示初心行人登正道之階梯。入泥洹之等級。尋者當愧為行之難成。毋鄙斯文之淺近也。若心稱言旨於一晌間。則智斷難量神解莫測。若虛搆文言情乖所說。空延歲月取證無由。事等貧人數他財寶。於己何益者哉

[0462c03]　　具緣第一　訶欲第二　棄蓋第三　調和第四　方便第五　正修第六　善發第七　覺魔第八治病第九　證果第十

简体字　　　　　正體字

and muddle-headed that they might advance onto the Path—it is easy to discourse on the subject, but difficult for them to implement the practice. How then could one justify launching into extensive discussions of the abstruse and marvelous?

II. The Doctrine Proper

  A. Ten Calming-and-Insight Concepts with Encouragement and Cautioning

    1. Encouragement

We shall now offer a general explanation of ten concepts in order to reveal to the novice practitioner the steps traversed in ascending along the orthodox Path as well as the stages involved in progressing toward entry into nirvāṇa. The investigator should adopt appropriate humility with regard to the difficulty of succeeding in cultivation and thus should not demean this text's shallowness and ready accessibility.

    2. Offering Cautionary Advice

If one's mind correctly gauges the import of these words, then, in the blink of an eye, one's qualities of wisdom and severance will become so great as to defy measurement and one's spiritual understanding will become unfathomably deep.

If, however, one disingenuously seizes on passages out of context or, due to personal sentiments, distorts the instructions of the text, then the months and years will be needlessly drawn out while actual realization will have no basis for development. One's circumstance then would be like that of the pauper who spends his time calculating the wealth of other men. What possible benefit could this have for oneself?

    3. Listing Sections and Revealing Their Aims

    a. Listing Section Titles

| | |
|---|---|
| First: | Fulfillment of Prerequisite Conditions |
| Second: | Renunciation of Desires |
| Third: | Elimination of the Hindrances |
| Fourth: | Making Adjustments |
| Fifth: | Implementation of Skillful Means |
| Sixth: | The Actual Cultivation |
| Seventh: | Manifestation of [Roots of] Goodness |
| Eighth: | Recognition of the Work of Demons |
| Ninth: | Treatment of Disorders |
| Tenth: | Realization of the Fruits |

[0462c07]　　今略举此十意。以明修止观者。此是初心学坐之急要。若能善取其意而修习之。可以安心免难。发定生解证于无漏之圣果也。

[0462c07]　　今略舉此十意。以明修止觀者。此是初心學坐之急要。若能善取其意而修習之。可以安心免難。發定生解證於無漏之聖果也。

简体字

正體字

b. CLARIFYING THE AIM OF THE SECTIONS

Now, we shall briefly treat these ten concepts in order to instruct the practitioner of calming-and-insight. These are crucial essentials for the beginner's training in sitting meditation. If one is well able to grasp their intent and thus proceed to cultivate them, one will be able to settle the mind, avoid difficulties, manifest meditative absorption, develop understanding, and achieve realization of the non-outflow fruits of the Ārya.

| 具缘第一 | 具緣第一 |
|---|---|
| [0462c11] 夫发心起行欲修止观者。要先外具五缘。第一持戒清净。如经中说。依因此戒。得生诸禅定及灭苦智慧。是故比丘应持戒清净。然有三种行人。持戒不同。一者若人未作佛弟子时不造五逆。后遇良师教受三归五戒为佛弟子。若得出家受沙弥十戒。次受具足戒作比丘比丘尼。从受戒来清净护持无所毁犯。是名上品持戒人也。当知是人修行止观必证佛法。犹如净衣易受染色。 | [0462c11] 夫發心起行欲修止觀者。要先外具五緣。第一持戒清淨。如經中說。依因此戒。得生諸禪定及滅苦智慧。是故比丘應持戒清淨。然有三種行人。持戒不同。一者若人未作佛弟子時不造五逆。後遇良師教受三歸五戒為佛弟子。若得出家受沙彌十戒。次受具足戒作比丘比丘尼。從受戒來清淨護持無所毀犯。是名上品持戒人也。當知是人修行止觀必證佛法。猶如淨衣易受染色。 |
| 简体字 | 正體字 |

# Chapter One

## Fulfillment of the Prerequisite Conditions

B. The Actual Exposition of the Ten Sections
1. Section One: Fulfillment of the Five Conditions
   a. Observing Precepts Purely
   1) Generally Clarifying Essentials of Precept Observance

Now, one who has resolved to begin practice and who desires to cultivate calming-and-insight must first fulfill five conditions related to outward circumstances. The first is the requirement that one maintain purity in practice of the moral precepts. This is as stated in a sutra: "It is in dependence upon and because of these moral precepts that one succeeds in developing the dhyāna absorptions as well as the wisdom which puts an end to suffering. Therefore the bhikshu should be pure in upholding the precepts."[1]

2) Specific Explanation of Features of Three Precept-Observance Levels
   a) Superior Level of Precept Observance

In this regard, there are three classes of practitioners according to differences in the upholding of precepts.

The first is as follows: Prior to becoming a disciple of the Buddha [this practitioner] did not commit any of the five relentless (*ānantarya*) transgressions.[2] Later he encountered a good master who taught him to accept the Three Refuges and the five precepts, whereby he became a disciple of the Buddha. If he succeeded in leaving the home life, he first took on the ten precepts of the *śrāmaṇera* and then later received the complete precepts, thereby becoming a bhikshu or, [in the case of a woman], a bhikshuni. From the time of first taking precepts, he has been pure in guarding and upholding them and thus has been entirely free of transgressions.

In the upholding of the precepts, this person is of the superior grade. One should understand that in cultivating calming-and-insight, such a person will certainly achieve realization in those dharmas of the Buddha. Such a person may be likened to a robe which is perfectly clean and which thus will easily absorb the appropriate dye.

二者若人受得戒已。虽不犯重。于诸轻戒多所毁损。为修定故即能如法忏悔。亦名持戒清净能生定慧。如衣曾有垢腻若能浣净染亦可着。三者若人受得戒已。不能坚心护持轻重诸戒。多所毁犯。依小乘教门即无忏悔四重之法。若依大乘教门犹可灭除。故经云。佛法有二种健人。一者不作诸恶。二者作已能悔。夫欲忏悔者。须具十法助成其忏。一者明信因果。二者生重怖畏。三者深起惭愧。四者求灭罪方法。所谓大乘经中明诸行法。应当如法修行。五者发露先罪。六者断相续心。

二者若人受得戒已。雖不犯重。於諸輕戒多所毀損。為修定故即能如法懺悔。亦名持戒清淨能生定慧。如衣曾有垢膩若能浣淨染亦可著。三者若人受得戒已。不能堅心護持輕重諸戒。多所毀犯。依小乘教門即無懺悔四重之法。若依大乘教門猶可滅除。故經云。佛法有二種健人。一者不作諸惡。二者作已能悔。夫欲懺悔者。須具十法助成其懺。一者明信因果。二者生重怖畏。三者深起慚愧。四者求滅罪方法。所謂大乘經中明諸行法。應當如法修行。五者發露先罪。六者斷相續心。

简体字　　　　　　　　　　正體字

b) Middling Level of Precept Observance

In the case of the second, after having received the precepts, although there have been no transgressions of the major precepts, still there has been much damage done to the minor prohibitions. If for the sake of cultivating meditative absorption, such a person is able forthwith to carry out repentance in a manner prescribed by Dharma, he too may qualify as one whose upholding of the precepts is pure and he, too shall be able to develop meditative absorption and wisdom. Such an individual may be compared to a robe which, although once soiled, has nonetheless been entirely cleaned such that dye will take in this case as well.

c) Inferior Level of Precept Observance
i) Repentance According to Methods of the Great Vehicle
(1) Clarification of Repentance Options in Great and Small Vehicles

In the case of the third, having received the precepts, one was unable to guard and uphold the precepts with a firm mind and thus there has been much transgression of both minor and major prohibitions. According to the approach of the Small Vehicle, there is no method whereby one may repent and be purified of transgressions against the four major monastic prohibitions. If, however, one resorts to the approach of the teachings of the Great Vehicle, there is still a means whereby these [karmic transgressions] may be extinguished.

(2) Citation of Evidence That One Who Repents Becomes a Healthy Person

Accordingly, a sutra notes: "Within the Buddha's Dharma, there are two types of healthy people: those who have committed no evil deeds whatsoever and those who, having committed them, have been able to repent of them."[3]

(3) Repentance According to Great Vehicle Methods
(a) Implementation Relying on Ten Repentance-Assisting Dharmas

Now, as for one seeking to repent, he must fulfill ten dharmas which assist the success of repentance:

First, develop a clear understanding and belief in cause-and-effect;
Second, give rise to profound fearfulness [of retribution];
Third, bring forth a deep sense of shame and dread of blame;[4]
Fourth, seek out a method to extinguish offenses. This refers to the methods of practice explained in the Great Vehicle sutras. One should cultivate them in accord with the Dharma;
Fifth, reveal and confess prior offenses;
Sixth, cut off the thought of continuing [the offenses];

七者起护法心。八者发大誓愿度脱众生。九者常念十方诸佛。十者观罪性无生。若能成就如此十法。庄严道场洗浣清净着净洁衣。烧香散花于三宝前如法修行。一七三七日。或一月三月。乃至经年专心忏悔。所犯重罪取灭方止。云何知重罪灭相。若行者如是至心忏悔时。自觉身心轻利得好瑞梦。或复覩诸。灵瑞异相。或觉善心开发。或自于坐中。觉身如云如影。因是渐证得诸禅境界。或复豁然解悟心生善识法相。随所闻经即知义趣。因是法喜心无忧悔。如是等种种因缘。当知即是破戒障道罪灭之相。从是已后坚持禁戒。亦名尸罗清净。

七者起護法心。八者發大誓願度脫眾生。九者常念十方諸佛。十者觀罪性無生。若能成就如此十法。莊嚴道場洗浣清淨著淨潔衣。燒香散花於三寶前如法修行。一七三七日。或一月三月。乃至經年專心懺悔。所犯重罪取滅方止。云何知重罪滅相。若行者如是至心懺悔時。自覺身心輕利得好瑞夢。或復覩諸。靈瑞異相。或覺善心開發。或自於坐中。覺身如雲如影。因是漸證得諸禪境界。或復豁然解悟心生善識法相。隨所聞經即知義趣。因是法喜心無憂悔。如是等種種因緣。當知即是破戒障道罪滅之相。從是已後堅持禁戒。亦名尸羅清淨。

简体字 正體字

Seventh, resolve to protect the Dharma;

Eighth, make the great vow to liberate beings;

Ninth, be ever mindful of all Buddhas of the ten directions;

Tenth, contemplate the nature of offenses as being unproduced.

### (i) Revealing Duration of Repentance Dharma

If one is able to completely carry out these ten dharmas, one should then proceed to adorn the site for cultivating the path, bathe one's body, clothe oneself in clean robes, burn incense and scatter flowers. Then, in front of the Triple Jewel, one should carry on the practice of repentance in accord with the Dharma, doing so for one week or three weeks, or perhaps for one month or three months, or perhaps even continuing on for years during which one repents single-mindedly of the grave offenses involved in transgressing the prohibitions. One should stop only when one has succeeded in extinguishing them.

### (ii) Revealing Signs Indicating Extinguishing of Offenses

How is one to recognize the signs that grave offenses have been extinguished?

It may be that, as the practitioner carries out sincere repentance in this fashion, he experiences his body and mind becoming light and pleasant, and also experiences a fine and auspicious dream.

It may be that he sees all manner of magical, auspicious, and rare signs. It may be that he becomes aware of his wholesome thoughts opening forth and developing. Or, while seated in meditation, he may become aware of his body as like a cloud or a shadow, and then, from this point on, he may gradually achieve realization of the mental states characteristic of the dhyānas.

It may be that he experiences the powerful and sudden arising of awakened thought whereby he is well able to recognize the marks of dharmas and is able to understand the meaning and connotation of whichever sutra he encounters, realizing from this Dharma bliss and a mind no longer beset by worry or regretfulness. All manner of causes and conditions such as these should be recognized as signs indicating that the path-obstructing offenses resulting from breaking the precepts have been extinguished.

### (iii) Clarification: Post-repentance Precept Observance Constitutes Purity

If, from this point on, one firmly upholds the restrictive prohibitions, this too qualifies as purity in *śīla* (moral virtue). Such a practitioner

可修禅定。犹如破坏垢腻之衣。若能补治浣洗清净犹可染着。若人犯重禁已恐障禅定。虽不依诸经修诸行法。但生重惭愧。于三宝前发露先罪。断相续心。端身常坐。观罪性空念十方佛。若出禅时即须至心烧香礼拜忏悔。诵戒及诵大乘经典。障道重罪自当渐渐消灭。因此尸罗清净禅定开发。故妙胜定经云。若人犯重罪已。心生怖畏欲求除灭。若除禅定馀无能灭。是人应当在空闲处摄心常坐。及诵大乘经。一切重罪悉皆消灭。诸禅三昧自然现前。第二衣食具足者。衣法有三种。一者如雪山大士。随得一衣蔽形

可修禪定。猶如破壞垢腻之衣。若能補治浣洗清淨猶可染著。若人犯重禁已恐障禪定。雖不依諸經修諸行法。但生重慚愧。於三寶前發露先罪。斷相續心。端身常坐。觀罪性空念十方佛。若出禪時即須至心燒香禮拜懺悔。誦戒及誦大乘經典。障道重罪自當漸漸消滅。因此尸羅清淨禪定開發。故妙勝定經云。若人犯重罪已。心生怖畏欲求除滅。若除禪定餘無能滅。是人應當在空閑處攝心常坐。及誦大乘經。一切重罪悉皆消滅。諸禪三昧自然現前。第二衣食具足者。衣法有三種。一者如雪山大士。隨得一衣蔽形

简体字        正體字

may be able to cultivate dhyāna absorption. He may be likened to a torn and deeply soiled robe which one has been able to patch and wash clean enough that it becomes capable of being dyed.

(b) Repentance According to the Great Vehicle's Signlessness Principle
(i) Explanation Proper.

If a person has transgressed against one of the major prohibitions, it is to be feared that this may obstruct acquisition of dhyāna absorption. Even though he may not be able to rely upon cultivating practice methods set forth in the Sutras, still, he may simply bring forth an intense sense of shame and dread of blame, go before the Triple Jewel, confess his former offenses, and cut off any thought of continuing them. He may then take up the practice of continuously engaging in seated meditation with his body erect, contemplating the nature of offenses as empty, and remaining mindful of the Buddhas of the ten directions.

Whenever he emerges from dhyāna, he must, with sincere mind, burn incense, bow in reverence, repent, and then recite the precepts and recite the Great Vehicle sutras as well. The grave offenses which obstruct the path should naturally and gradually become extinguished. On account of this, his *śīla* becomes pure and thus dhyāna absorption may develop.

(ii) Citation of Evidence

Accordingly, the *Sutra on the Marvelous and Superior Meditative Absorption* states, "If, after a person has transgressed against a major precept, his mind becomes beset by fearfulness and he thus wishes to extinguish it, there is no other means aside from dhyāna absorption which can be successful in extinguishing it.

"In a deserted and quiet place, this person should focus his mind and engage in the practice of continuously sitting in meditation while also proceeding to recite the Great Vehicle sutras. All of the grave offenses will be entirely extinguished and each of the dhyāna absorptions will naturally manifest."[5]

b. Ensuring Adequacy of Clothing and Food
1) Clothing
a) Superior-Roots Clothing

As for the second, the requirement that clothing and food be adequate, there are three approaches with regard to clothing: The first is as exemplified by the Great Master of the Snowy Mountains[6] who happened to obtain a single cloak adequate to cover up his body

即足。以不游人间堪忍力成故。二者如迦叶常受头陀法。但畜粪扫三衣不畜馀长。三者若多寒国土。及忍力未成之者。如来亦许三衣之外。畜百一等物。而要须说净知量知足。若过贪求积聚则心乱妨道。次食法有四种。一者若上人大士。深山绝世。草果随时得资身者。二者常行头陀受乞食法。是乞食法。能破四种邪命。依正命自活。能生圣道故。邪命自活者。一下口食。二仰口食。三维口食。四方口食。邪命之相。如舍利弗为青目女说。

即足。以不遊人間堪忍力成故。二者如迦葉常受頭陀法。但畜糞掃三衣不畜餘長。三者若多寒國土。及忍力未成之者。如來亦許三衣之外。畜百一等物。而要須說淨知量知足。若過貪求積聚則心亂妨道。次食法有四種。一者若上人大士。深山絕世。草果隨時得資身者。二者常行頭陀受乞食法。是乞食法。能破四種邪命。依正命自活。能生聖道故。邪命自活者。一下口食。二仰口食。三維口食。四方口食。邪命之相。如舍利弗為青目女說。

简体字               正體字

and took that to be adequate because he never encountered people and additionally had perfected the ability to endure the elements.

### b) MIDDLING-ROOTS SUSTENANCE

The second category is that exemplified by Mahākāśyapa who, because he always cultivated the *dhūta* practices,[7] wore only a single three-part rag robe and accumulated no other clothing.

### c) INFERIOR-ROOTS CLOTHING

The third category relates to countries where the weather is often cold and to individuals whose endurance abilities are not yet perfected. In these cases the Tathāgata also permitted the accumulation of a hundred and one other things aside from the three-part robe. However it was necessary to purify them verbally,[8] to refrain from being excessive, and to be satisfied with the appropriate amount. Were one to allow oneself to overindulge by being acquisitive and desirous of accumulating things, then the mind would become disrupted and they would become an obstacle to the Path. [463b]

### 2) SUSTENANCE
### a) SUPERIOR-ROOTS SUSTENANCE

Next, as for the categories relating to food, there are four, the first of which is that exemplified by the superior man and great master who, having entirely severed relations with the world, dwells deep in the mountains, eating the native herbs and fruits according to the season, thus supplying the requirements of the body.

### b) MIDDLING-ROOTS SUSTENANCE

As for the second, he always cultivates the *dhūta* practice of accepting only food which has been obtained on the alms round. Through the practice of accepting only alms food, one is able to curb four types of wrong livelihood. One relies exclusively upon right livelihood to maintain life because he is thereby able to bring forth the path of the Āryas.

As for the types of wrong livelihood, they are: first, obtaining sustenance through inferiorly-directed endeavors; second, obtaining sustenance through upwardly-directed endeavors; third, obtaining sustenance through endeavors directed at the midpoints; and fourth, obtaining sustenance through endeavors focused on the directions. The characteristics of inappropriate livelihood are as explained by Śāriputra to Śucimukhī.[9]

三者阿兰若处。檀越送食。四者于僧中洁净食。有此等食缘具足。名衣食具足。何以故。无此等缘则心不安隐于道有妨。第三得闲居静处。闲者不作众事名之为闲。无愦闹故名之为静。有三处可修禅定。一者深山绝人之处二者头陀兰若之处。离于聚落极近三四里。此则放牧声绝无诸愦闹。三者远白衣住处清净伽蓝中。皆名闲居静处。第四息诸缘务。有四意。一息治生缘务。不作有为事业。二息人间缘务。不追寻俗人朋友亲戚知识。断绝人事往还。

三者阿蘭若處。檀越送食。四者於僧中潔淨食。有此等食緣具足。名衣食具足。何以故。無此等緣則心不安隱於道有妨。第三得閑居靜處。閑者不作眾事名之為閑。無憒鬧故名之為靜。有三處可修禪定。一者深山絕人之處二者頭陀蘭若之處。離于聚落極近三四里。此則放牧聲絕無諸憒鬧。三者遠白衣住處清淨伽藍中。皆名閑居靜處。第四息諸緣務。有四意。一息治生緣務。不作有為事業。二息人間緣務。不追尋俗人朋友親戚知識。斷絕人事往還。

简体字                               正體字

c) INFERIOR-ROOTS SUSTENANCE

The third involves residing in an *araṇya* (hermitage) where a *dānapati* brings offerings of food. The fourth is where one lives among the Sangha and eats pure food. Where one has the advantage of sustenance arrangements such as these, then this is what is meant by achieving adequacy in food and clothing. Why is this? If one does not have circumstances such as these, the mind will not be at peace and thus this will act as an obstacle to the Path.

c. [OBTAINING EASEFUL AND QUIET DWELLING]

The third [among the five prerequisite conditions] requires that one find an easeful and quiet dwelling place. One who is in a state of ease is not working at doing manifold tasks and so this is what we mean when we stipulate "easeful." A "quiet" place is one in which there is no commotion whatsoever. There are three types of places where one may be able to cultivate dhyāna absorption.

1) [REMOTE DWELLING]

The first is deep in the mountains in a place cut off from people.

2) [ARAṆYA DWELLING]

The second is an *araṇya* dedicated to *dhūta* practices no closer than a mile or so (lit. "three or four *li*") from a village.[10] In such a case, the noise of cattle will be cut off and there will be no commotion.

3) [SAṄGHĀRĀMA DWELLING]

The third is within the confines of a pure *saṅghārāma* (monastic dwelling) far from the residences of laypeople. All of these circumstances may serve as "easeful and quiet dwelling places."

d. [PUTTING RESPONSIBILITIES TO REST]

The fourth [of the five prerequisite conditions] is that one put all responsibilities to rest. This involves four specific ideas:

1) [CESSATION OF LIVELIHOOD]

First, one must put to rest responsibilities relating to making a living and must not engage in endeavors associated with ordinary conditioned existence.

2) [CESSATION OF RELATIONSHIPS]

Second, one must put to rest all interpersonal responsibilities. One must not seek out ordinary people, friends, relatives, or acquaintances. One must cut off all endeavors involving interactions with other people.

三息工巧技术缘务。不作世间工匠技术医方。禁呪卜相书数算计等事。四息学问缘务。读诵听学等悉皆弃舍。此为息诸缘务。所以者何。若多缘务。则行道事癈心乱难摄。第五近善知识。善知识有三。一外护善知识。经营供养善能将护行人不相恼乱。二者同行善知识。共修一道互相劝发不相扰乱。三者教授善知识。以内外方便禅定法门示教利喜。略明五种缘务竟

三息工巧技術緣務。不作世間工匠技術醫方。禁呪卜相書數算計等事。四息學問緣務。讀誦聽學等悉皆棄捨。此為息諸緣務。所以者何。若多緣務。則行道事癈心亂難攝。第五近善知識。善知識有三。一外護善知識。經營供養善能將護行人不相惱亂。二者同行善知識。共修一道互相勸發不相擾亂。三者教授善知識。以內外方便禪定法門示教利喜。略明五種緣務竟

简体字          正體字

3) [CESSATION OF ACTIVITIES]

Third, one must put to rest all responsibilities relating to arts or crafts and must not pursue any activities involving skilled worldly trades, art, medicine, occult mantra-related activities, physiognomy, writing, accounting, making calculations, and other such matters.

4) [CESSATION OF STUDY]

Fourth, one must put to rest all responsibilities relating to learning. One must put aside reading, reciting, listening, studying, and so forth. This is what is meant by putting all responsibilities to rest. Why is this necessary? If one is involved in many responsibilities, then matters related to cultivating the Path will deteriorate. The mind will become disturbed and difficult to focus.

e. [DRAWING NEAR TO GOOD SPIRITUAL FRIENDS]

The fifth [of the five prerequisite conditions] requires that one draw near to good spiritual friends. Good spiritual friends are of three types:

1) [EXTERNALLY-PROTECTIVE GOOD SPIRITUAL FRIENDS]

The first is the "externally-protective" good spiritual friend who provides necessary provisions, makes offerings, and is well able to take care of the practitioner's needs, doing so in a fashion which precludes any mutual disturbance.

2) [IDENTICAL-PRACTICE GOOD SPIRITUAL FRIENDS]

The second is the "identical-practice" good spiritual friend together with whom one cultivates a single path. Each provides the other with encouragement and inspiration while refraining from mutual bother or disturbance.

3) [INSTRUCTIVE GOOD SPIRITUAL FRIENDS]

The third is the "instructive" good spiritual friend who instructs and delights the practitioner with teachings about the internal and external skillful means associated with the Dharma entryway of dhyāna absorption. This is the conclusion of the summary clarification of the five kinds of necessary prerequisites.

| 简体字 | 正體字 |
|---|---|
| 诃欲第二<br><br>[0463b27]　所言诃欲者。谓五欲也。凡欲坐禅修习止观。必须诃责。五欲者。是世间色声香味触。常能诳惑一切凡夫令生爱着。若能深知过罪。即不亲近是名诃欲。一诃色欲者。所谓男女形貌端严。修目长眉朱唇素齿。及世间宝物。青黄赤白红紫缥绿。种种妙色能令愚人见则生爱作诸恶业。如频婆娑罗王。以色欲故身入敌国。在婬女阿梵波罗房中。优填王以色染故截五百仙人手足。如此等种种过罪。二诃声欲者。所谓箜篌筝笛。丝竹金石音乐之声。及男女歌咏赞诵等声。能令凡夫 | 訶欲第二<br><br>[0463b27]　所言訶欲者。謂五欲也。凡欲坐禪修習止觀。必須訶責。五欲者。是世間色聲香味觸。常能誑惑一切凡夫令生愛著。若能深知過罪。即不親近是名訶欲。一訶色欲者。所謂男女形貌端嚴。修目長眉朱唇素齒。及世間寶物。青黃赤白紅紫縹綠。種種妙色能令愚人見則生愛作諸惡業。如頻婆娑羅王。以色欲故身入敵國。在婬女阿梵波羅房中。優填王以色染故截五百仙人手足。如此等種種過罪。二訶聲欲者。所謂箜篌箏笛。絲竹金石音樂之聲。及男女歌詠讚誦等聲。能令凡夫 |

# CHAPTER TWO
## Renunciation of Desires

As for what is meant by "renunciation of desires," this refers to the five objects of sensual desire (*kāmacchanda*). When one wishes to cultivate calming-and-insight while sitting in dhyāna meditation, it is absolutely essential to renounce them. The "five desires" are the forms, sounds, smells, tastes and touchables encountered in the world. They are ever able to deceive and delude all ordinary people, causing them to develop fond attachment. If one is able to become deeply aware of the negative consequences of desires, one will not become involved with them. This is what is meant by renouncing desire.

### 1) [DESIRE FOR FORMS]

First, the renunciation of the desire for forms refers to such forms as the stately and decorous shapes and features of men and women, including alluring eyes, long eyebrows, red lips, and white teeth, as well as things regarded in the world as precious. It also includes colors such as blue, yellow, red, white, vermilion, purple, chartreuse, and green. All sorts of such marvelous forms are able to influence the foolish observer to develop fondness for them and consequently embark on all manner of unwholesome karmic deeds.

One example is King Bimbisāra who, on account of sexual desire, stole into a hostile kingdom and entered the quarters of Āmrapālī, the courtesan. Another is King Udayana who, corrupted by lust, hacked off the hands and feet of five hundred rishis. [Desire for forms] is possessed of all manner of negative consequences like this.

### 2) [DESIRE FOR SOUNDS]

Second, the renunciation of the desire for sounds, refers to musical sounds such as issue from harps, zithers, or flutes, and such as are created by strings, bamboo, metal, or stone, and refers also to such sounds as the voices of men and women singing, chanting, hymning, or reciting. They may influence the foolish common person

闻即染着起诸恶业。如五
百仙人雪山住。闻甄陀罗
女歌声。即失禅定心醉狂
乱。如是等种种因缘。知
声过罪。三诃香欲者。所
谓男女身香。世间饮食馨
香及一切薰香等。愚人不
了香相。闻即爱着开结使
门。如一比丘在莲华池
边。闻华香气心生爱乐。
池神即大诃责。何故偷我
香气。以着香故令诸结使
卧者皆起。如是等种种因
缘。知香过罪。四诃味欲
者。所谓苦酸甘辛咸淡
等。种种饮食肴膳美味。
能令凡夫心生染着起不善
业。如一沙弥染着酪味。
命终之后生在酪中受其虫
身。如是等种种因缘。知
味过罪。五诃触欲者。男
女身分柔软细滑。

who hears them to straightaway develop defiling attachment and to generate all manner of unwholesome karmic deeds.

One example of this phenomenon is the case of the five hundred rishis dwelling in the Snow Mountains who heard the singing of a *kinnara*-spirit maiden, immediately lost dhyāna absorption, and thus became mentally intoxicated and deranged.[1] On account of all sorts of reasons such as these, one should realize the negative consequences of desire for sounds.

### 3) [DESIRE FOR FRAGRANCES]

Third, the renunciation of the desire for fragrances, refers to the physical scents of men and women, the fragrances of human society's food, drink and perfumes, as well as all manner of incenses and aromas. An ordinary fool does not understand the true character of fragrances and so, on smelling them, becomes fondly attached, and thus opens the door to the fetters.[2]

An example of this is the case of the bhikshu at the side of the lotus pond who smelled the fragrance of the blossoms and whose thoughts were then moved to fondness and pleasure. The pond spirit then rebuked him soundly by scolding, "Why did you steal my fragrances?"[3]

One may, on account of attachment to fragrances, stir up otherwise quiescent fetters. For all sorts of reasons like these, one should realize the negative consequences of the desire for fragrances.

### 4) [DESIRE FOR FLAVORS]

Fourth, the renunciation of the desire for flavors, refers to bitterness, sourness, sweetness, pungency, saltiness, mildness, and other such fine flavors characteristic of fine beverages and cuisine. They may be able to incite the foolish common person to develop a kind of corrupting attachment and then to consequently engage in unwholesome karma.

An example of this is the case of the *śrāmaṇera* who developed a corrupting obsession with the flavor of curds and who thus, at the conclusion of his life, was reborn in a container of curds where he took on the body of a curd worm.[4] On account of all manner of reasons such as these, one should realize the negative consequences of the desire for flavors.

### 5) [DESIRE FOR TOUCHABLES]

Fifth, the renunciation of the desire for touchables, refers to the softness and delicate slickness of the bodies of men and women, to the

寒时体温热时体凉。及诸好触。愚人无智为之沈没起障道业。如一角仙。因触欲故遂失神通。为婬女骑颈。如是等种种因缘。知触过罪。如上诃欲之法。出摩诃衍论中说。复云哀哉众生常为五欲所恼。而犹求之不已。此五欲者得之转剧。如火益薪其焰转炽。五欲无乐如狗啮枯骨。五欲增诤如鸟竞肉。五欲烧人如逆风执炬。五欲害人如贱毒蛇。五欲无实如梦所得。五欲不久假借须臾如击石火。智者思之亦如怨贼。世人愚惑贪着五欲至死不舍。后受无量苦恼。此五欲法与畜生同有。

sensations of their physical warmth when it is cold, their physical coolness when it is hot, as well as to all other pleasant tactile contacts. The foolish person, lacking in wisdom, is submerged by them and thus generates karma blocking progress along the Path.

An example of this was the one-horned rishi who, on account of indulging the desire for physical contact, lost the superknowledges and ended up with a courtesan riding him about, mounted atop his shoulders.[5] For all manner of reasons such as these, one should realize the negative consequences of the desire for touchables.

  b.  [SCRIPTURAL CITATIONS]

The dharma of renouncing desire as treated above is drawn from the discussion in the *Mahāyāna Treatise*.[6]

It additionally states, "Alas! These beings! They are constantly harassed by the five desires and yet they continue to pursue them incessantly.

"As for these five types of desire, gaining their objects results in their becoming even more intense.

"They are like fire which, when stoked with more firewood, burns ever brighter.

"The five desires yield no happiness. [When one pursues them], one is comparable to a dog gnawing away at a dried-up bone.

"The five desires proliferate contention, just as birds skirmish over carrion.

"The five desires scorch a person, just as one is burned when carrying a torch into the wind.

"The five desires bring harm to a person, just as when one treads upon a poisonous snake.

"Like bounty gained in a dream, the five desires have nothing real about them.

"[The pleasure arising from] the five desires does not endure long. It is borrowed only for a moment and is like a spark struck from a stone.

"The wise also consider them to be like enemies or thieves. The worldly person is foolish and deluded, is covetously attached to the five desires, won't relinquish them even in the face of death, and later undergoes immeasurable suffering and aggravation as a result.

"This dharma of the five desires is something people have in common with animals."[7]

| | |
|---|---|
| 一切众生常为五欲所使。名欲奴仆。坐此弊欲沈堕三涂。我今修禅复为障蔽。此为大贼急当远之。如禅经偈中说 | 一切眾生常為五欲所使。名欲奴僕。坐此弊欲沈墮三塗。我今修禪復為障蔽。此為大賊急當遠之。如禪經偈中說 |

| | | | |
|---|---|---|---|
| 生死不断绝 | 贪欲嗜味故 | 生死不斷絕 | 貪欲嗜味故 |
| 养冤入丘冢 | 虚受诸辛苦 | 養冤入丘塚 | 虛受諸辛苦 |
| 身臭如死尸 | 九孔流不净 | 身臭如死屍 | 九孔流不淨 |
| 如厕虫乐粪 | 愚人身无异 | 如廁蟲樂糞 | 愚人身無異 |
| 智者应观身 | 不贪染世乐 | 智者應觀身 | 不貪染世樂 |
| 无累无所欲 | 是名真涅盘 | 無累無所欲 | 是名真涅槃 |
| 如诸佛所说 | 一心一意行 | 如諸佛所說 | 一心一意行 |
| 数息在禅定 | 是名行头陀 | 數息在禪定 | 是名行頭陀 |

| | |
|---|---|
| 简体字 | 正體字 |

All beings typically act under the direction of the five desires and thus become slaves to the desires. On account of this, having become covered over by desires, they are prone to fall into the three lower realms.

[One should reflect]: "If, even as I cultivate dhyāna meditation, I revert to being obstructed and covered over by them, then I am a great thief. I must urgently distance myself from them."

As stated in verses from the *Dhyāna Sutra*:

That birth and death are not cut off
Is on account of desire and fondness for its flavor.
As when nursing a grudge all the way to the grave,
One endures in vain all manner of bitter suffering.

The smell of the body is like that of a corpse.
Impurities stream forth from its nine apertures.
Just as worms in an outhouse delight in the feces,
So too does the foolish man delight in the body.

The one who is wise should contemplate the body,
And not lust after the tainted pleasures of the world.
To be without burdens and to have nothing desired—
This is what qualifies as true nirvāṇa.

It's just as described by the Buddhas themselves:
Practicing with one mind and singular intention,
While counting the breath in dhyāna absorption—
It is this which is the practice of the *dhūtas* (ascetic practices).[8]

## 弃盖第三

[0464a15]　　所言弃盖者。谓五盖也。一弃贪欲盖。前说外五尘中生欲。今约内意根中生欲。谓行者端坐修禅。心生欲觉念念相续。覆盖善心。令不生长觉已应弃。所以者何。如术婆伽欲心内发。尚能烧身。况复心生欲火而不烧诸善法。贪欲之人去道甚远。所以者何。欲为种种恼乱住处。若心着欲无由近道。如除盖偈说

| | |
|---|---|
| 入道惭愧人 | 持钵福众生 |
| 云何纵尘欲 | 沈没于五情 |
| 已舍五欲乐 | 弃之而不顾 |
| 如何还欲得 | 如愚自食吐 |
| 诸欲求时苦 | 得时多怖畏 |

简体字

---

## 棄蓋第三

[0464a15]　　所言棄蓋者。謂五蓋也。一棄貪欲蓋。前說外五塵中生欲。今約內意根中生欲。謂行者端坐修禪。心生欲覺念念相續。覆蓋善心。令不生長覺已應棄。所以者何。如術婆伽欲心內發。尚能燒身。況復心生欲火而不燒諸善法。貪欲之人去道甚遠。所以者何。欲為種種惱亂住處。若心著欲無由近道。如除蓋偈說

| | |
|---|---|
| 入道慚愧人 | 持鉢福眾生 |
| 云何縱塵欲 | 沈沒於五情 |
| 已捨五欲樂 | 棄之而不顧 |
| 如何還欲得 | 如愚自食吐 |
| 諸欲求時苦 | 得時多怖畏 |

正體字

## Chapter Three

### Elimination of the Hindrances

3. Section Three: Elimination of the Hindrances

As for "elimination of the hindrances," it refers to the five hindrances (*nīvaraṇa*, *āvaraṇa*).[1]

a. [The Hindrance of Desire]

The first involves the eliminating of the hindrance of sensual desire (*kāmachanda*). Earlier, we discussed the outward arising of desire with respect to the five sense objects. Now we are concerned with the inward arising of desire in the intellectual mind faculty. This refers to instances where the practitioner is seated upright, cultivating dhyāna meditation, and his mind generates continuously, one after another, desire-based ideations which cover over the wholesome mind, preventing it from developing. When one realizes that this is occurring, one should eliminate [such ideation].

Why should he do so? If, as in the case of Śubhakara,[2] the internal arising of the lustful mind is able even to burn the body, how could it be that all wholesome dharmas would not be burned up as well when the mind generates the fire of desire? Persons possessed by desire are extremely far away from the Path.[3] How is this so? Desire is the dwelling place of all manner of affliction-based disturbances. If the mind becomes attached and beset by desire, there is no way for one to grow near to the Path. This is as explained in "Verse on Eliminating the Hindrances":

> The person knowing shame and blame who's entered the Path
> Takes up his bowl and provides merit for beings.
> How could one give free reign to desire for sense objects
> And become immersed in the five senses?
>
> Having already renounced the pleasures of the five desires,
> One has cast them off and does not look back.
> Why would one still desire to gain them,
> Like a fool who laps up his own vomit?
>
> All desires are suffering at the time they are sought.
> When gained, one is usually fearful [of losing them].

失时怀热恼　一切无乐处
诸欲患如是　以何能舍之
得深禅定乐　即不为所欺

[0464b01] 二弃瞋恚盖。瞋是失佛法之根本。坠恶道之因缘。法乐之冤家善心之大贼。种种恶口之府藏。是故行者于坐禅时思惟。此人现在恼我及恼我亲。赞叹我冤。思惟过去未来亦如是。是为九恼。故生瞋恨。瞋恨故生怨。以怨心生故便起心恼。彼如是瞋觉覆心。故名为盖。当急弃之无令增长。如释提婆那以偈问佛

何物杀安乐　何物杀无忧
何物毒之根　吞灭一切善

[0464b10] 佛以偈答言

杀瞋则安乐　杀瞋则无忧
瞋为毒之根　瞋灭一切善

[0464b13] 如是知已。当修慈忍以灭除之。令心清净。

简体字

正體字

On losing them, one experiences burning aggravation.
At every point there's nowhere where pleasure abides.

Given that desires are so attended by troubles,
How might one be able to relinquish them?
If one but gains the bliss of deep dhyāna absorption,
One will then no longer be subject to their deception.

### b. [THE HINDRANCE OF ILL WILL]

The second is the elimination of the hindrance of ill will (*vyāpāda*). Ill will is the basis for losing the Buddha Dharma, a cause and condition for falling into the wretched destinies,[4] the nemesis of Dharma bliss, the great thief which preys on the wholesome mind, and the repository of all manner of abusive speech.

Accordingly, when the practitioner is sitting in dhyāna meditation, he might think to himself, "This fellow is now tormenting me. What's more, he torments my relatives and praises my adversaries." Continuing, he might think, "It's been like this in the past as well, and it will continue to be so in the future. This amounts to a nine-fold torment."

Consequently, he might become full of ill will and, based upon that ill will, he might begin to cherish animosity. On account of generating animosity, he might then think to torment the other individual. In this fashion, ill will serves to cover over the mind and, for this reason, [this "hindrance" is also] referred to as a "covering." One should proceed urgently to eliminate it and should not allow it to proliferate. This is as illustrated by Śakra Devānām Indra's query which he posed to the Buddha in verse:

What thing is it which, killed, brings peace and brings bliss?
What thing is it which, slain, brings freedom from worry?
What thing is it which is the root of venomousness,
And which devours and destroys all forms of goodness?

The Buddha responded, speaking in verse:

If one kills anger (*krodha*), one becomes peaceful and happy.
If one slays anger, one becomes free of one's worries.
It is anger which is the root of venomousness.
It is anger which destroys all forms of goodness.[5]

Having realized this, one should cultivate kindness and patience as the means to dispel anger so that the mind may become pure.

64

The Essentials of Buddhist Meditation

三弃睡眠盖。内心昏暗名
为睡。五情暗蔽放恣。支
节委卧睡熟为眠。以是因
缘名为睡眠。盖能破今世
后世实乐法心。及后世生
天及涅盘乐。如是恶法最
为不善。何以故。诸馀盖
情觉故可除。睡眠如死无
所觉识。以不觉故难可除
灭。如佛诸菩萨诃睡眠弟
子。偈曰

汝起勿抱臭尸卧
种种不净假名人
如得重病箭入体
诸苦痛集安可眠

如人被缚将去杀
灾害垂至安可眠

结贼不灭害未除
如共毒蛇同室居
亦如临阵两刃间
尔时云何安可眠

眠为大暗无所见
日日欺诳夺人明
以眠覆心无所见
如是大失安可眠

简体字

三棄睡眠蓋。內心昏闇名
為睡。五情闇蔽放恣。支
節委臥睡熟為眠。以是因
緣名為睡眠。蓋能破今世
後世實樂法心。及後世生
天及涅槃樂。如是惡法最
為不善。何以故。諸餘蓋
情覺故可除。睡眠如死無
所覺識。以不覺故難可除
滅。如佛諸菩薩訶睡眠弟
子。偈曰

汝起勿抱臭屍臥
種種不淨假名人
如得重病箭入體
諸苦痛集安可眠

如人被縛將去殺
災害垂至安可眠

結賊不滅害未除
如共毒蛇同室居
亦如臨陣兩刃間
爾時云何安可眠

眠為大闇無所見
日日欺誑奪人明
以眠覆心無所見
如是大失安可眠

正體字

c. [THE HINDRANCE OF LETHARGY-AND-SLEEPINESS]

Third, eliminating the hindrance of lethargy-and-sleepiness (*styāna-middha*).[6] "Lethargy" (*styāna*) refers to a dullness and dimness of the subjective mental processes, whereas "sleepiness" (*middha*) refers to the state in which the five sense faculties are so covered over by dimness that the control of the limbs is relinquished and one curls up and sleeps soundly. It is for this reason that [this "hindrance" is also] referred to as the "covering" of sleep.

It is capable of destroying the mind intent on Dharma which generates genuine bliss in this and later lives and is also capable of destroying the bliss derived in later lives from rebirth in the heavens and the realization of nirvāṇa. An unwholesome dharma such as this is the very worst. How is this so? Unlike the mental states associated with the other hindrances which may be expelled simply by becoming aware of their presence, sleep is like being dead in that an aware state of consciousness is no longer present. Because one is not abiding in a state of awareness, this remains a difficult thing to eliminate.

This is as described in a verse employed by buddhas and bodhisattvas to reprimand somnolent disciples:

Get up! Don't lie there hugging that stinking corpse.
It's but various impurities falsely designated as a "person."
It's as if you've gotten a serious disease or been shot by an arrow.
With such an accumulation of suffering and pain, how could you
    sleep?

[The entire world is burned up by the fire of death.
When you should be seeking to escape, how could you sleep?][7]
You're like a man in shackles being led to his execution.
With disastrous harm so imminent, how could you sleep?

The thieves of the fetters haven't been destroyed and their harm
    has not yet been eliminated.
It's as if one were sharing a room with a venomous serpent.
It's also as if one were entering a battle's gauntlet of swords.
What would you do then? How could you sleep?

Sleep amounts to a vast darkness where one can't see anything.
Every day it deceives and steals away a person's clarity.
Because sleep covers over the mind, one can't see anything.
As it has such great drawbacks, how could you sleep?

[0464b27] 如是等种种因缘。诃睡眠盖。警觉无常。减损睡眠。令无昏覆。若昏睡心重。当用禅镇杖却之。四弃掉悔盖。掉有三种。一者身掉。身好游走诸杂戏谑。坐不暂安。二者口掉。好喜吟咏竞诤是非。无益戏论世间语言等。三者心掉。心情放逸。纵意攀缘。思惟文艺世间才技诸恶觉观等名为心掉。掉之为法破出家人。心如人摄心犹不能定。何况掉散。掉散之人如无钩醉象穴鼻骆驼不可禁制。如偈说

[0464b27] 如是等種種因緣。訶睡眠蓋。警覺無常。減損睡眠。令無昏覆。若昏睡心重。當用禪鎮杖却之。四棄掉悔蓋。掉有三種。一者身掉。身好遊走諸雜戲謔。坐不暫安。二者口掉。好喜吟咏競諍是非。無益戲論世間語言等。三者心掉。心情放逸。縱意攀緣。思惟文藝世間才技諸惡覺觀等名為心掉。掉之為法破出家人。心如人攝心猶不能定。何況掉散。掉散之人如無鉤醉象穴鼻駱駝不可禁制。如偈說

简体字                                          正體字

For all manner of reasons such as these, one remonstrates against the hindrance of sleepiness. One becomes alarmed by and awakened to impermanence, pares down one's need for sleep and prevents oneself from being covered over by its dullness. If the mind becomes severely afflicted with dullness and sleep, one should resort to a dhyāna wake-up device or staff to get rid of them.[8]

   d. [THE HINDRANCE OF EXCITEDNESS-AND-REGRETFULNESS]

The fourth, eliminating the hindrance of excitedness-and-regretfulness (*auddhatya-kaukṛtya*).[9]

   1) [EXCITEDNESS]

As for excitedness itself (*auddhatya*), there are three types:

   a) [PHYSICAL EXCITEDNESS]

The first is physical excitedness which is characterized by the body's habitual enjoyment of wandering about engaging in all manner of foolishness while having no ability to feel even momentarily peaceful when sitting down.

   b) [VERBAL EXCITEDNESS]

The second type is verbal excitedness which is characterized by the habitual enjoyment of singing, chanting, disputation over rights and wrongs, useless and frivolous discourse, the discussion of worldly matters, and so forth.

   c) [MENTAL EXCITEDNESS]

The third type is mental excitedness. Here, one's mental inclination is towards neglectfulness and towards indulging the mind in its manipulation of circumstances. This may involve musing over literature, the arts, worldly talents and artisanship, as well as all manner of unwholesome ideation and discursive thought. These are characteristic features of mental excitedness.

The function of excitedness as a dharma is to destroy the mind of the monastic. Even if a person strives to focus his thoughts, he might still be unable to develop meditative absorption, how much the less so if he falls prey to excitedness and scatteredness. Someone under the influence of excitedness and scatteredness is like a drunken elephant unrestrained by the trainer's hook and like a camel without a nose ring. None of these are subject to control or discipline. This is as described in a verse:

汝已剃头着染衣
执持瓦钵行乞食
云何乐着戏掉法
放逸纵情失法利

[0464c09] 既失法利又失世乐。觉其过已当急弃之。悔者悔能成盖。若掉无悔则不成盖。何以故。掉时未在缘中故。后欲入定时方悔。前所作忧恼覆心故名为盖。但悔有二种。一者因掉后生悔如前所说。二者如作大重罪人常怀怖畏。悔箭入心坚不可拔。如偈说

不应作而作　应作而不作
悔恼火所烧　后世堕恶道
若人罪能悔　悔已莫复忧
如是心安乐　不应常念着

简体字

---

汝已剃頭著染衣
執持瓦鉢行乞食
云何樂著戲掉法
放逸縱情失法利

[0464c09] 既失法利又失世樂。覺其過已當急棄之。悔者悔能成蓋。若掉無悔則不成蓋。何以故。掉時未在緣中故。後欲入定時方悔。前所作憂惱覆心故名為蓋。但悔有二種。一者因掉後生悔如前所說。二者如作大重罪人常懷怖畏。悔箭入心堅不可拔。如偈說

不應作而作　應作而不作
悔惱火所燒　後世墮惡道
若人罪能悔　悔已莫復憂
如是心安樂　不應常念著

正體字

You've already shaved your head and donned the dyed robe.
Taking up the clay bowl, you go out on the alms round.
How then can you delight in and be attached to dharmas of
  frivolity and excitedness?
Being neglectful and giving rein to your inclinations, you lose the
  benefits of Dharma.[10]

Since one loses the benefits of Dharma, one loses worldly bliss as
well. Having realized one's errors, one should strive with urgency
to eliminate [the excitedness hindrance].

  2) [REGRETFULNESS]

As for regretfulness (*kaukṛtya*), it is regretfulness itself which brings
about the creation of a hindrance in this context. If one merely
experiences instances of excitedness in which there is no operative
regretfulness, this situation is not one wherein a [true] hindrance
has been created. How is this the case? It is because at such times of
experiencing excitedness [pure and simple], one may not yet have
become involved in objective conditions. However, later, when one
is desirous of entering meditative absorption, one may then experience regretfulness over what one may actually have done. Then
worry-based afflictions cover over the mind. It is on account of this
that there is the creation of a "covering" [hindrance].

  a) [TWO TYPES OF REGRETFULNESS]

Regretfulness itself is of two types. The first is regretfulness which
arises as a consequence of excitedness as explained above. The
second is exemplified by the person who has committed a major
and severe offense and who thus constantly experiences feelings of
fearfulness. The arrow of regretfulness has entered his mind and
has become stuck so firmly that it can not be pulled out. This is as
described in a verse:

Through having done what one shouldn't have done,
Or through having failed to do what one should have done,
One is burned by the fire of the regretfulness affliction,
And, in a later life, falls into the wretched destinies.

If a person is able to feel regret for an offense,
Then, having regretted it, he should not continue to feel troubled.
In this way, the mind can be peaceful and happy.
One should not constantly seize upon it through recollection.

若有二种悔　　若应作不作
不应作而作　　是则愚人相

不以心悔故　　不作而能作
诸恶事已作　　不能令不作

[0464c23] 五弃疑盖者。以疑
覆心故。于诸法中不得信
心。信心无故于佛法中空
无所获。譬如有人入于宝
山。若无有手无所能取。
然则疑过甚多未必障定。
今正障定疑者有三种。一
者疑自。而作是念我诸根
暗钝。罪垢深重非其人
乎。自作此疑。定法终不
得发。若欲修定勿当自
轻。以宿世善根难测故。
二者疑师。彼人威仪相貌
如是。自尚无道何能教
我。作是疑慢即为障定。
欲除之法如摩诃衍论中
说。如臭皮囊中金。以贪
金故。不可弃其臭囊。行
者亦尔。师虽不

简体字

若有二種悔　　若應作不作
不應作而作　　是則愚人相

不以心悔故　　不作而能作
諸惡事已作　　不能令不作

[0464c23] 五棄疑蓋者。以疑
覆心故。於諸法中不得信
心。信心無故於佛法中空
無所獲。譬如有人入於寶
山。若無有手無所能取。
然則疑過甚多未必障定。
今正障定疑者有三種。一
者疑自。而作是念我諸根
闇鈍。罪垢深重非其人
乎。自作此疑。定法終不
得發。若欲修定勿當自
輕。以宿世善根難測故。
二者疑師。彼人威儀相貌
如是。自尚無道何能教
我。作是疑慢即為障定。
欲除之法如摩訶衍論中
說。如臭皮囊中金。以貪
金故。不可棄其臭囊。行
者亦爾。師雖不

正體字

If one possesses either of the two kinds of regretfulness,
Whether it be over having failed to do what one should have done,
Or over having done what one should not have done,
This is the mark of a stupid person.

It is not the case that, on account of being regretful,
One will somehow be able to do what one failed to do.
All of the ill deeds which one has already committed
Can't be caused thereby to become undone.[11]

e.   [The Hindrance of Doubt]

Fifth, eliminating the hindrance of doubt. Because doubt covers over the mind, one is unable to develop faith in any dharma. Because one has no mind of faith, one encounters the Buddha's Dharma in vain and gains nothing from it. This is analogous to a man's entering into a mountain of jewels. If he has no hands, he is unable to acquire anything at all.

This being the case, the faults of doubt are extremely numerous. Still, they need not necessarily obstruct the acquisition of meditative absorption. Now, as for those sorts of doubt which may directly obstruct meditative absorption, they are of three types:

1)   [Doubt in Oneself]

The first is where one doubts oneself and thus thinks to himself, "All of my faculties are all dim and dull. The defilement from my previous offenses is deep and severe. Could it be that I'm not the man for this?" If one indulges in creating these doubts, then the dharma of meditative absorption will never be able to manifest. If one desires to cultivate meditative absorption, one must not slight oneself, for it is difficult to fathom the extent of one's roots of goodness planted in former lifetimes.

2)   [Doubt in One's Guru]

The second type of doubt is that wherein one doubts one's own guru, thinking, "If his deportment and appearance are such as this, he must not have any realization of the Path. How then could he be able to teach me?" If one develops such doubting arrogance, then it constitutes an obstruction to meditative absorption.

A method for one wishing to be rid of this [hindrance] is mentioned in the *Mahāyāna Treatise*: "This is comparable to when gold is encased in a smelly leather pouch."[12] Because one wishes to possess the gold, one can't just pitch out the smelly pouch. The practitioner's situation may be just like this. Although the guru may not

清净。亦应生佛想。三疑
法。世人多执本心。于所
受法不能即信敬心受行。
若心生犹豫即法不染心。
何以故。疑障之义如偈中
说

| | |
|---|---|
| 如人在岐路 | 疑惑无所趣 |
| 诸法实相中 | 疑亦复如是 |
| 疑故不勤求 | 诸法之实相 |
| 见疑从痴生 | 恶中之恶者 |
| 善不善法中 | 生死及涅盘 |
| 定实真有法 | 于中莫生疑 |
| 汝若怀疑惑 | 死王狱吏缚 |
| 如师子㧅鹿 | 不能得解脱 |
| 在世虽有疑 | 当随喜善法 |
| 譬如观岐道 | 利好者应逐 |

[0465a18]　佛法之中信为能
入。若无信者虽在佛法终
无所获。如是种种因缘。
觉知疑过当急弃之。

简体字

---

清淨。亦應生佛想。三疑
法。世人多執本心。於所
受法不能即信敬心受行。
若心生猶豫即法不染心。
何以故。疑障之義如偈中
說

| | |
|---|---|
| 如人在岐路 | 疑惑無所趣 |
| 諸法實相中 | 疑亦復如是 |
| 疑故不勤求 | 諸法之實相 |
| 見疑從癡生 | 惡中之惡者 |
| 善不善法中 | 生死及涅槃 |
| 定實真有法 | 於中莫生疑 |
| 汝若懷疑惑 | 死王獄吏縛 |
| 如師子搏鹿 | 不能得解脫 |
| 在世雖有疑 | 當隨喜善法 |
| 譬如觀岐道 | 利好者應逐 |

[0465a18]　佛法之中信為能
入。若無信者雖在佛法終
無所獲。如是種種因緣。
覺知疑過當急棄之。

正體字

be immaculate, still, one should look upon him as one would look upon the Buddha.

3) [DOUBT IN THE DHARMA]

The third type of doubt is that wherein one doubts the Dharma. Worldly people are usually attached to their own ideas and thus are not able to immediately believe the Dharma which they have received, thus accepting it and cultivating it with a respectful mind. If the mind becomes hesitant, then, even though one has immediate exposure to the Dharma, it makes no imprint on the mind. Why is this the case? It is because doubt hinders it. The concept is as described in a verse:

It's just as when a person stands at a fork in the road
And is so deluded by doubt that he goes nowhere at all.
In relation to [fathoming] the true character of dharmas,
Doubt functions in precisely the very same way.

Because one has doubts, one doesn't diligently seek
[Realization of] the true character of dharmas.
View-filled doubts arise from delusion.
Among all of the ills, they are the very worst.

As for good versus unwholesome dharmas,
[The dharmas of] birth-and-death and nirvāṇa,
And dharmas which are definitely genuine and truly valid,
One must not indulge any doubts about them.

If you cherish the delusion of doubt,
The King of Death's hell messengers will tie you up.
Just as when a lion pounces on a deer,
You'll be unable then to achieve liberation.

Although whilst living in the world, one may have one's doubts,
One should still happily accord with wholesome dharmas,
Just as when one contemplates a fork in the road,
One should follow that path which is most beneficial.[13]

In the Dharma of the Buddha, it is through faith that one gains entry. If one has no faith, then, although in the presence of the Buddha's Dharma, he will finally gain nothing whatsoever from it. Based on all sorts of reasons such as these, one realizes the faults inhering in doubtfulness. Thus one should urgently strive to eliminate it.

问曰不善法广尘数无量。何故但弃五法。答曰此五盖中即具有三毒等分。四法为根本。亦得摄八万四千诸尘劳门。一贪欲盖。即贪毒。二瞋恚盖。即瞋毒。三睡眠及疑。此二法是痴毒。四掉悔即是等分摄合为四分。烦恼一中有二万一千。四中合为八万四千。是故除此五盖。即是除一切不善之法。行者如是等种种因缘弃于五盖。譬如负债得脱。重病得差。如饥饿之人得至豐国如于恶贼中得自免济。安隐无患。行者亦如是。除此五盖。其心安隐清凉快乐。如日月以五事覆翳烟尘云雾罗睺阿修罗手障。则不能明照。人心五盖亦复如是

問曰不善法廣塵數無量。何故但棄五法。答曰此五蓋中即具有三毒等分。四法為根本。亦得攝八萬四千諸塵勞門。一貪欲蓋。即貪毒。二瞋恚蓋。即瞋毒。三睡眠及疑。此二法是癡毒。四掉悔即是等分攝合為四分。煩惱一中有二萬一千。四中合為八萬四千。是故除此五蓋。即是除一切不善之法。行者如是等種種因緣棄於五蓋。譬如負債得脫。重病得差。如饑餓之人得至豐國如於惡賊中得自免濟。安隱無患。行者亦如是。除此五蓋。其心安隱清涼快樂。如日月以五事覆翳煙塵雲霧羅睺阿修羅手障。則不能明照。人心五蓋亦復如是

简体字　　　　　　正體字

f. [QUESTION: WHY ONLY GET RID OF FIVE?]

**Question:** Unwholesome dharmas are vast in number and the sense objects are countless. Why is it that one must only get rid of five dharmas?

1) [REPLY: ALL ARE SUBSUMED]

**Reply:** These five hindrances basically take four dharmas as their foundation, namely the three poisons as well as instances of "equal-distribution" [in relation to those three poisons.] These in turn subsume all eighty-four thousand points of entry into toilsome involvement with sense objects. First, the hindrance of desire is just synonymous with the poison of desire. Second, the hindrance of ill will is just synonymous with the poison of anger. Third, the two categories of dharmas consisting of lethargy-and-sleepiness and doubtfulness are just synonymous with the poison of delusion. The fourth is excitedness-and-regretfulness. It belongs to the "equal-distribution" category.

Together, these constitute the four categories of afflictions. In each of them, there are twenty-one thousand. In all four of them, there are collectively a total of eighty-four thousand. Hence, when one gets rid of these five hindrances, one thereby eliminates all unwholesome dharmas. Based on all manner of reasons such as these, the practitioner strives to eliminate the five hindrances.

g. [BENEFITS OF ELIMINATING THE HINDRANCES]

The practitioner is like a person who has gained freedom from a debt or one who has been cured of a serious disease, like a starving man arriving in a prosperous country, or like one who has been rescued safe and unharmed from a band of villains. When he eliminates these five hindrances, his mind becomes calm and secure and he feels clear, cool, and blissful.

Just as with the sun and moon which may be obscured and prevented from shining brightly by the five phenomena of smoke, dust, clouds, fog and the hand of the *asura* known as Rāhu, so it is as well with the human mind and the five "covering" hindrances.[14]

调和第四

[0465b05]　　　夫行者初学坐禅。欲修十方三世佛法者。应当先发大誓愿。度脱一切众生。愿求无上佛道。其心坚固犹如金刚。精进勇猛不惜身命。若成就一切佛法终不退转。然后坐中正念思惟一切诸法真实之相。所谓善不善无记法。内外根尘妄识。一切有漏烦恼法。三界有为生死因果法。皆因心有。故十地经云。三界无别有。唯是一心作。若知心无性则诸法不实。心无染着则一切生死业行止息。作是观已。乃应如次起行修习也。云何名调和。今借近譬以况斯法。如世间陶师欲造众器。先须善巧调泥。令使不彊不懦。然后可就轮绳。

简体字

調和第四

[0465b05]　　　夫行者初學坐禪。欲修十方三世佛法者。應當先發大誓願。度脱一切眾生。願求無上佛道。其心堅固猶如金剛。精進勇猛不惜身命。若成就一切佛法終不退轉。然後坐中正念思惟一切諸法真實之相。所謂善不善無記法。內外根塵妄識。一切有漏煩惱法。三界有為生死因果法。皆因心有。故十地經云。三界無別有。唯是一心作。若知心無性則諸法不實。心無染著則一切生死業行止息。作是觀已。乃應如次起行修習也。云何名調和。今借近譬以況斯法。如世間陶師欲造眾器。先須善巧調泥。令使不彊不懦。然後可就輪繩。

正體字

# CHAPTER FOUR
## Making Adjustments

4. SECTION FOUR: MAKING ADJUSTMENTS

a. PRELIMINARY CONSIDERATIONS

Now, when the practitioner first takes up the study of sitting in dhyāna meditation, as one who wishes to cultivate the Dharma of the Buddhas of the ten directions and the three periods of time, he should first make the great vows to bring all beings to liberation. In vowing to pursue the unsurpassed way of the Buddhas, he makes his mind as solid as *vajra* and resolves to be industrious and courageous to the point that he will not even spare his own life and will never retreat from his quest to perfect all buddha dharmas.

Next, seated in meditation and employing right mindfulness, he deliberates on the true character of dharmas. These include those dharmas commonly referred to as: wholesome, unwholesome and karmically neutral; the inward and outward sense faculties and sense objects; the error-ridden consciousnesses; and all of the dharmas associated with outflow-impurities and afflictions. They also include the conditioned dharmas throughout the three realms and the dharmas of cause-and-effect associated with cyclic births and deaths. [He observes that] they all exist solely on the basis of mind.

Accordingly, the *Sutra on the Ten Grounds* states, "Throughout the three realms, there is nothing else at all. It is all created solely from the mind."[1] If one realizes that mind is devoid of [any inherently-existent] nature, then [one realizes as well that] all dharmas are not genuinely real. If the mind becomes free of defiling attachment, then all of the karmic activity in the sphere of birth-and-death comes to a halt. After one has carried out this contemplation, he should then take up the cultivation according to the proper sequence.

What is meant by "making adjustments?" Now, to draw upon familiar subjects as analogies for this dharma, it is just as when a common potter wishes to create various sorts of vessels. He must first skillfully make adjustments in the clay such that it is neither too stiff nor too soft. Afterwards he may move to the potter's wheel.

亦如弹琴前应调弦。令宽
急得所。方可入弄出诸妙
曲。行者修心亦复如是。
善调五事必使和适。则三
昧易生。有所不调多诸妨
难。善根难发。一调食
者。夫食之为法。本欲资
身进道。食若过饱则气
急。身满百脉不通。令心
闭塞坐念不安。若食过少
则。身羸心悬意虑不固此
二皆非得定之道。若食秽
触之物。令人心识昏迷。
若食不宜之物则动宿病。
使四大违反。此为修定之
初。须深慎之也。故经云
身安则道隆。饮食知节
量。常乐在空闲。心静乐
精进。是名诸佛教。二调
睡眠者。夫眠是无明惑
覆。不可纵之。若其眠寐
过多非唯废

亦如彈琴前應調絃。令寬
急得所。方可入弄出諸妙
曲。行者修心亦復如是。
善調五事必使和適。則三
昧易生。有所不調多諸妨
難。善根難發。一調食
者。夫食之為法。本欲資
身進道。食若過飽則氣
急。身滿百脈不通。令心
閉塞坐念不安。若食過少
則。身羸心懸意慮不固此
二皆非得定之道。若食穢
觸之物。令人心識昏迷。
若食不宜之物則動宿病。
使四大違反。此為修定之
初。須深慎之也。故經云
身安則道隆。飲食知節
量。常樂在空閑。心靜樂
精進。是名諸佛教。二調
睡眠者。夫眠是無明惑
覆。不可縱之。若其眠寐
過多非唯廢

简体字                                                正體字

It is also like playing the lute. One should first make adjustments to the strings, properly setting their tension. Then one may proceed to play, producing all sorts of marvelous melodies.

When the practitioner cultivates the mind, it is just the same. One must make skillful adjustments in five different matters and must make those adjustments appropriately. Then samādhi will develop easily. If there is some factor which has not been properly adjusted, then there will be all sorts of obstructive difficulties and it will be hard for roots of goodness to develop.

b. [ADJUSTMENTS IN FOOD]

First, making adjustments with respect to food. Now, as for food's function as a dharma, basically it is consumed out of a desire to supply the body so that one may advance along the Path. If one eats to the point of becoming too full, then the breathing will be strained, the body will feel stuffed, the energetic channels will not flow freely, the mental faculties will be blocked up, and, when sitting, one's thoughts will not be tranquil.

If one eats too little, the body will waste away, the mind will be too tightly strung, and mental deliberation will be unstable. Neither of these two situations is the way to the realization of meditative absorption.

If one consumes contaminated food, then it will cause a person's mind consciousness to become dull and confused. If one consumes foods which are not appropriate, then it will stimulate all sorts of dormant residual disorders to arise and will cause the four great elements to be thrown far out of balance.

This is the beginning phase of one's cultivation of meditative absorption. Thus one must be extremely careful in the way one proceeds. In this connection, we have [two] scriptural citations:

If the body is content, the Path may flourish.

If one maintains awareness of proper measure in food and drink,
If one is always happy abiding in a remote abode, and
If, with the mind stilled, one finds happiness in diligent effort—
This accords with the teachings of all buddhas.[2]

c. [ADJUSTMENTS IN SLEEP]

The second involves adjustments in sleep. Now sleep is a matter of being covered over by a state of ignorance and delusion. One must not give free rein to it. If one sleeps too much, one not only wastes

修圣法。亦复丧失功夫。而能令心暗昧善根沈没。当觉悟无常调伏睡眠。令神气清白念心明净。如是乃可栖心圣境三昧现前。故经云。初夜后夜亦勿有废。无以睡眠因缘。令一生空过无所得也。当念无常之火烧诸世间。早求自度勿睡眠也。三调身。四调息。五调心。此三应合用不得别说。但有初中后。方法不同是则入住出相有异也。夫初欲入禅调身者。行人欲入三昧调身之宜。若在定外行住进止。动静运为。悉须详审。若所作麁犷则气息随麁。以气麁故则心散难录。兼复坐时烦愦心不恬怡。身虽在定外

修聖法。亦復喪失功夫。而能令心闇昧善根沈沒。當覺悟無常調伏睡眠。令神氣清白念心明淨。如是乃可棲心聖境三昧現前。故經云。初夜後夜亦勿有廢。無以睡眠因緣。令一生空過無所得也。當念無常之火燒諸世間。早求自度勿睡眠也。三調身。四調息。五調心。此三應合用不得別說。但有初中後。方法不同是則入住出相有異也。夫初欲入禪調身者。行人欲入三昧調身之宜。若在定外行住進止。動靜運為。悉須詳審。若所作麁獷則氣息隨麁。以氣麁故則心散難錄。兼復坐時煩憒心不恬怡。身雖在定外

简体字　　　　　　　　正體字

the opportunity to cultivate the Dharma of the Āryas, but one also destroys any meditative skill. Thus one may cause the mind to be cloaked in darkness and the roots of goodness to become entirely submerged.

One should awaken to the import of impermanence, regulate and subdue sleep, cause one's spiritual energy to be clear, and one's mindful thought to be bright and pure. In this way, one will establish one's mind in the mental state of the Āryas and cause samādhi to manifest before one.

Accordingly, a sutra states, "Nor should there be any wasted time in either the first or last phases of the night.... One must not, on account of sleep, cause a lifetime to pass by emptily with nothing whatsoever achieved. One should remain mindful that the fire of impermanence burns up the entire world. Thus one should seek early on to bring about one's own deliverance. One must not indulge [a tendency to enjoy] sleep."[3]

#### d. [ADJUSTMENTS IN BODY, BREATH, AND MIND]

The third, adjustments in the body, the fourth, adjustments in the breath, and the fifth, adjustments in the mind—these three ought to be considered together. They cannot be discussed separately. However, there are differences in technique at the beginning, middle, and end. This being the case, there are differences in their features when entering into, abiding in, and coming out of a session.

##### 1) [ADJUSTMENTS WHEN ENTERING MEDITATION]
##### a) [ADJUSTMENTS IN THE BODY WHEN ENTERING MEDITATION]
##### i) [IMPORTANT PHYSICAL CONSIDERATIONS WHEN NOT MEDITATING]

Now, as for the physical adjustments undertaken when one first desires to enter dhyāna, there are issues of appropriateness in the physical adjustments undertaken by the cultivator wishing to enter samādhi. For instance, when one is abiding outside of meditative absorption, whether walking, standing, commencing an activity, or stopping one, whether moving or still—it is essential to be meticulously attentive in all such situations.

If one's actions are coarse and impetuous, then one's breath will become correspondingly coarse. Because the breath is coarse, then the thoughts will become scattered and difficult to register clearly. Additionally, when one returns to sitting, he will be agitated and muddled and the mind will not be tranquil or contented. Even though one's body may not be abiding in a state of meditative

亦须用意。逆作方便后入禅时。须善安身得所。初至绳床即须先安坐处。每令安稳久久无妨。次当正脚。若半跏坐以左脚置右脚上。牵来近身。令左脚指与右髀齐。右脚指与左髀齐。若欲全跏即正右脚置左脚上。次解宽衣带周正。不令坐时脱落。次当安手以左手掌置右手上。重累手相对顿置左脚上。牵来近身当心而安。次当正身先当挺动其身并诸支节。作七八反如似按摩法。勿令手足差异。如是已则端直。令脊骨勿曲勿耸。次正头颈令鼻与脐相对。不偏

亦須用意。逆作方便後入禪時。須善安身得所。初至繩床即須先安坐處。每令安穩久久無妨。次當正脚。若半跏坐以左脚置右脚上。牽來近身。令左脚指與右髀齊。右脚指與左髀齊。若欲全跏即正右脚置左脚上。次解寬衣帶周正。不令坐時脫落。次當安手以左手掌置右手上。重累手相對頓置左脚上。牽來近身當心而安。次當正身先當挺動其身并諸支節。作七八反如似按摩法。勿令手足差異。如是已則端直。令脊骨勿曲勿聳。次正頭頸令鼻與臍相對。不偏

简体字                                    正體字

absorption, still, it is essential to employ one's mind to implement skillful means in a counteractive manner [preventing any such disturbance of tranquility].

ii) [Physical Adjustments When Beginning the Meditation Session]

(1) [Sitting Down]

Later, when one enters into dhyāna, it is essential to be skillful in stabilizing the body properly. When one first arrives at the sitting cushion, one must first establish oneself in the sitting location in such a manner that all is peaceful and secure so that nothing will interfere with remaining for a long time.

(2) [Arranging the Feet]

Next, one should arrange the feet correctly. If one is sitting in the half-lotus posture, one places the left foot so that it is on top of the right leg and then pulls it in so that it is close to the body proper. In doing so, one causes the toes of the left foot to become aligned with the right thigh while the toes of the right foot become aligned with the left thigh. If one wishes to sit in full lotus, one next corrects the arrangement of the right foot so that it rests atop the left leg.

(3) [Arranging Clothing]

Next, one loosens the belt on one's robe, making sure that it is straight all around and cannot fall open while one is sitting.

(4) [Arranging the Hands]

Next, one should arrange the hands. One lays the open left hand on top of the right hand so that they fit together and rest atop the left foot [in the case of half lotus]. One then draws them in toward the body so that they are centered and stable.

(5) [Consolidating the Posture]

Next, one should properly arrange the body, first making sure that the body is erect, and then seeing also that the limbs are set symmetrically, moving them back and forth as many as seven or eight times, as if massaging them into place. One must not allow the hands or feet to slip out of correct posture. Having done this, one then sits up perfectly straight, ensuring that the spine is neither slumping nor thrust forward.

(6) [Lining Up Head, Neck; Sitting Straight Up]

Next, one should straighten up the head and neck so that the nose and the navel are lined up and so that the head is not tilted to the

不斜。不低不昂。平面正住。次当口吐浊气吐气之法开口放气。不可令麁急。以之绵绵恣气而出。想身分中百脉不通处。放息随气而出。闭口鼻纳清气。如是至三。若身息调和但一亦足。次当闭口唇齿才相拄着。舌向上齶。次当闭眼才令断外光而已。当端身正坐。犹如奠石。无得身首四肢切尔摇动。是为初入禅定调身之法。举要言之。不宽不急是身调相。四初入禅调息法者。息有四种相。一风二喘三气四息。前三为不调相。后一为调相。云何为风相。坐时则鼻中息出入觉有声是风也。

简体字

不斜。不低不昂。平面正住。次當口吐濁氣吐氣之法開口放氣。不可令麁急。以之綿綿恣氣而出。想身分中百脈不通處。放息隨氣而出。閉口鼻納清氣。如是至三。若身息調和但一亦足。次當閉口唇齒纔相拄著。舌向上齶。次當閉眼纔令斷外光而已。當端身正坐。猶如奠石。無得身首四肢切爾搖動。是為初入禪定調身之法。舉要言之。不寬不急是身調相。四初入禪調息法者。息有四種相。一風二喘三氣四息。前三為不調相。後一為調相。云何為風相。坐時則鼻中息出入覺有聲是風也。

正體字

side, held at an angle, drooped downward, or raised upward. One faces forward and remains straight.

(7) [Preparing the Breath]

(a) [Expelling the Turbid]

Next, one should expel the turbid breath. The method for expelling the breath requires that one open the mouth and release the breath while not allowing this process to be either coarse or urgent. One should make it soft and smooth as one releases the breath and sends it forth. One should imagine that, throughout the body, any blockages within the numerous energetic pathways are moved on out as one exhales.

(b) [Inhaling the Pure]

Then, one closes the mouth and inhales pure breath through the nose. One should do this up to three times. If the physical respiration is already correctly adjusted, then only once is adequate.

(8) [Lips, Tongue, Eyes, Spine]

Next, one should close the mouth such that the lips and teeth are held together while the tongue is held up against the hard palate. Then one should close the eyes only enough that they block off the light from outside. One should straighten up the body and sit upright like a stele. One cannot allow the body, the head or the four limbs to move about even slightly.

iii) [Summary]

This is the technique for making physical adjustments as one first proceeds to enter dhyāna absorption. To speak of what is most essential, being neither too loose nor too tight is the mark of correct physical adjustment.

b) [Adjustments in Breath When Entering Meditation]

Fourth, the technique for making adjustments in the breath when first entering dhyāna meditation. The breath may possess any of four characteristics: first, windy breathing; second, uneven breathing; third, normal breathing; and fourth, subtle respiration. The first three are indications of inadequate adjustment, whereas the last one is characteristic of correct adjustment.

i) [Types of Breathing]

(1) [Windy Breathing]

What is meant by "windy" breathing? When one is sitting and one senses the presence of a sound as the breath comes into and goes forth from the nose this is "windy" breathing.

云何喘相。坐时息虽无声
而出入结滞不通是喘相
也。云何气相。坐时息虽
无声亦不结滞而出入不细
是气相也。云何息相。不
声不结不麁。出入绵绵若
存若亡。资神安隐情抱悦
豫。此是息相也。守风则
散。守喘则结。守气则
劳。守息即定。坐时有风
喘气三相。是名不调而用
心者。复为心患。心亦难
定。若欲调之当依三法。
一者下着安心。二者宽放
身体。三者想气。遍毛孔
出入通同无障。若细其心
令息微微然。息调则众患
不生。其心易定。

云何喘相。坐時息雖無聲
而出入結滯不通是喘相
也。云何氣相。坐時息雖
無聲亦不結滯而出入不細
是氣相也。云何息相。不
聲不結不麁。出入綿綿若
存若亡。資神安隱情抱悅
豫。此是息相也。守風則
散。守喘則結。守氣則
勞。守息即定。坐時有風
喘氣三相。是名不調而用
心者。復為心患。心亦難
定。若欲調之當依三法。
一者下著安心。二者寬放
身體。三者想氣。遍毛孔
出入通同無障。若細其心
令息微微然。息調則眾患
不生。其心易定。

简体字　　　　　　正體字

(2) [UNEVEN BREATHING]

What is meant by "uneven" breathing? When one is sitting and, even though the breath makes no sound, there is still a catching and halting such that it does not move on through, this is "uneven" breathing.

(3) [ORDINARY BREATHING]

What is meant by "ordinary" breathing? When one is sitting, even though the breath makes no sound and there is no catching and stopping, still, it is not subtle. This is "ordinary" breathing.

(4) [SUBTLE BREATHING]

What is meant by "subtle" respiration? There is no sound, no catching, and no coarseness. The exhalation and inhalation of the breath are smooth and of extended duration such that they are as if still there, and yet as if they have disappeared. This circumstance supports the spirit's abiding in peacefulness and stability. One feels pleased and content. These are the marks of subtle respiration.

ii) [EFFECTS OF EACH BREATH TYPE]

If one maintains windy breathing, then one becomes scattered. If one maintains uneven breathing, then one becomes stuck. If one maintains ordinary breathing, then one becomes weary. If one maintains subtle respiration, then one enters meditative absorption.

If, when one is sitting, there occur any of the three characteristics of windy breathing, uneven breathing, or ordinary breathing, these are indications of inadequate adjustment. In a case where one applies mental effort under these circumstances, they also bring about mental disturbance and make it difficult for the mind to enter meditative absorption.

iii) [ADJUSTMENT TECHNIQUES]

If one wishes to correct them, then one should rely on three techniques: First, stabilize the mind by anchoring it below, [at the navel]; second, relax and release the body; and third, visualize the breath penetrating through to all of the pores, going forth and coming in without any obstructions whatsoever. If one makes one's mind subtle, one causes the breath to become very fine. If the breath becomes regulated, then the manifold disorders do not arise. One's mind easily enters meditative absorption.

是名行者初入定时调息方法。举要言之。不澁不滑是调息相也。五初入定时调心者。有三义。一入二住三出。初入有二义。一者调伏乱想不令越逸。二者当令沈浮宽急得所。何等为沈相。若坐时心中昏暗无所记录。头好低垂。是为沈相。尔时当系念鼻端。令心住在缘中无分散意此可治沈。何等为浮相。若坐时心好飘动身亦不安。念外异缘此是浮相。尔时宜安心向下。系缘脐中制诸乱念。心即定住则心易安静。举要言之不沈不浮。是心调相。其定心亦有宽急之相。定心急

是名行者初入定時調息方法。舉要言之。不澁不滑是調息相也。五初入定時調心者。有三義。一入二住三出。初入有二義。一者調伏亂想不令越逸。二者當令沈浮寬急得所。何等為沈相。若坐時心中昏暗無所記錄。頭好低垂。是為沈相。爾時當繫念鼻端。令心住在緣中無分散意此可治沈。何等為浮相。若坐時心好飄動身亦不安。念外異緣此是浮相。爾時宜安心向下。繫緣臍中制諸亂念。心即定住則心易安靜。舉要言之不沈不浮。是心調相。其定心亦有寬急之相。定心急

简体字                                       正體字

iv) [Summary]

This constitutes the practitioner's technique for regulating the breath when first entering meditative absorption. To speak of the essentials, it is neither coarse nor "slippery."[4] This is the mark of regulated breathing.

c) [Adjustments in the Mind When Entering Meditation]

Fifth, the adjustment of the mind when first entering meditative absorption involves three concepts: first, entering; second, abiding; and third, emerging. The first, entering, involves two ideas.

i) [Disordered Thinking]

The first is the regulation and control of disordered thinking so that one's thoughts are not allowed to run off.

ii) [Sinking, Floating, Urgency, Laxity]

As for the second, one must cause conditions involving "sinking," "floating," "laxity," and "urgency" to regain correct adjustment.

(1) [Sinking]

What constitutes the mark of "sinking"? If when one is sitting, one's mental state is murky and dim, if one doesn't remember anything, or if one's head tends to droop downward, these all constitute marks of "sinking." At such a time, one should anchor one's mindfulness at the tip of the nose and thus compel one's mind to abide in the midst of objective conditions so that there will be no breaking up and scattering of the mental focus. This technique is able to counter "sinking."

(2) [Floating]

What are the indicators of "floating"? If while one is sitting, the mind prefers to drift off and move about, if the body, too, is ill at ease, or if one brings to mind various outward objective conditions, these are all marks of "floating." It is appropriate at such a time to stabilize the mind by directing it downwards and anchoring it at the navel, thus controlling chaotic thinking. The mind then immediately abides in stability. This being the case, it is then easy to establish the mind in stillness.

To speak of the essentials, it is being neither sinking nor floating which is the mark of the regulated mind.

(3) [Urgency]

The meditating mind may also possess marks of laxity or urgency. As for the marks of the meditating mind afflicted with the "urgency"

病相者。由坐中摄心用念。因此入定是故上向。胸臆急痛当宽放其心想。气皆流下患自差矣。若心宽病相者。觉心志散慢身好透迤。或口中涎流或时暗晦。尔时应当歛身急念。令心住缘中。身体相持以此为治心。有濇滑之相推之可知。是为初入定调心方法。夫入定本是从麁入细。是以身既为麁。息居其中。心最为细静。调麁就细令心安静。此则入定初方便也。是名初入定时调二事也。二住坐中调三事者。行人当于一坐之时随时长短。十二时或经一时。或至二三时。摄念用心。是中应须善识

病相者。由坐中攝心用念。因此入定是故上向。胸臆急痛當寬放其心想。氣皆流下患自差矣。若心寬病相者。覺心志散慢身好透迤。或口中涎流或時闇晦。爾時應當歛身急念。令心住緣中。身體相持以此為治心。有濇滑之相推之可知。是為初入定調心方法。夫入定本是從麁入細。是以身既為麁。息居其中。心最為細靜。調麁就細令心安靜。此則入定初方便也。是名初入定時調二事也。二住坐中調三事者。行人當於一坐之時隨時長短。十二時或經一時。或至二三時。攝念用心。是中應須善識

简体字　　　　正體字

malady, they arise from a situation where one has focused the mind and has brought mindfulness to bear. Because of this, one has entered a state of meditative absorption. Based on this circumstance, [the focus of one's attention] has moved upward and brought about intense pain in the chest. One should relax and release his mental focus downward. The subtle energetic breath will then all flow on down. If one were to do this, then the disturbance would naturally be cured.

(4) [LAXITY]

As for the marks of mind afflicted with the "laxity" malady, one realizes that one's mental determination has become scattered and dilatory and that one's body has tended to become slack and slumped. It may even be that there has been a flow of saliva from the mouth. At times, one may be dull and unclear. At such a time, one should draw up the body and make one's mindfulness more urgent. One should compel the mind to abide in the midst of objective conditions while compelling the body to maintain correct posture. One uses this technique to counter [laxity in] the mind.

In the event that the characteristics of being either rough or slippery manifest, if one infers from this, [the appropriate corrective actions] will become obvious. These constitute the techniques for regulating the mind when one first enters meditative absorption.

2) [SUMMARY OF ENTRY-RELATED ISSUES]

Now, entering meditative absorption is fundamentally a process wherein one proceeds from the coarse to enter the subtle. This is on account of the fact that the body is relatively coarse, the breath abides within it, and it is the mind which is the most subtle and still. Thus one's adjustments move from the coarse to that which is subtle, thereby causing the mind to become stable and still. These then are the initial skillful means involved in entering meditative absorption. This is what constitutes the regulation of the three[5] matters as one first enters meditative absorption.

3) [ADJUSTMENTS WHEN ABIDING IN MEDITATION]

Second: As for the regulation of the three matters that takes place as one abides in the sitting posture, the practitioner should apply his mind in the focusing of mindfulness whether the given session of sitting meditation is long or short and whether it extends for one, two, or three of the twelve two-hour periods in a day. One must clearly recognize the characteristics which indicate whether or not

身息心三事调不调相。若
坐时向虽调身竟。其身或
宽或急或偏或曲或低或
昂。身不端直。觉已随
正。令其安隐中无宽急。
平直正住。复次一坐之
中。身虽调和而气不调
和。不调和相者。如上所
说。或风或喘。或复气
急。身中胀满当用前法随
而治之。每令息道绵绵如
有如无。次一坐中身息虽
调。而心或浮沈宽急不
定。尔时若觉当用前法调
令中适。此三事的无前
后。随不调者而调适之。
令一坐之中。身息及心三
事。调适无相乖越。和融
不二

身息心三事調不調相。若
坐時向雖調身竟。其身或
寬或急或偏或曲或低或
昂。身不端直。覺已隨
正。令其安隱中無寬急。
平直正住。復次一坐之
中。身雖調和而氣不調
和。不調和相者。如上所
說。或風或喘。或復氣
急。身中脹滿當用前法隨
而治之。每令息道綿綿如
有如無。次一坐中身息雖
調。而心或浮沈寬急不
定。爾時若覺當用前法調
令中適。此三事的無前
後。隨不調者而調適之。
令一坐之中。身息及心三
事。調適無相乖越。和融
不二

简体字                正體字

the three phenomena of body, breath, and mind are in a state of correct adjustment.

    a) [THE BODY]

As one continues with a given session of sitting, if, even though one has already finished making adjustments to the body, it nonetheless occurs that the body becomes either lax or tense, either tilted or crooked, or either drooped or arched upward, so that the body is not upright and straight—as soon as one becomes aware of it, one must then correct it. One must ensure that, as one abides in peacefulness and stability, one remains free of any laxity or urgency, and that one remains in a posture which is level, straight, and upright.

    b) [THE BREATH]

Then again, during a single session of sitting, although the body may be correctly adjusted, the breath may still not be in harmony. The marks of its not being regulated are as discussed above. Perhaps there is "windy" breathing. Perhaps there is "uneven" breathing. Or perhaps, in addition, the breathing has become so urgent that there is a sense within the body of distention and fullness. In such cases, one should employ the previously discussed methods and thus counter them accordingly. In every case, one should cause the breath-channel phenomena to manifest in a smooth and continuous manner, while seeming to be as if present and yet not present.

    c) [THE MIND]

Again, it may be that in the course of a single session of sitting, although the body and the breath are correctly regulated, still, the mind may have failed to achieve meditative absorption on account of being either "floating," "sinking," "lax," or "urgent." At such a time, when one becomes aware of it, one should employ the previously mentioned regulating techniques to cause it to abide appropriately in between [such extremes].

    4) [SUMMARY OF ABIDING-RELATED ISSUES]

These three matters most definitely do not have any fixed sequence of implementation. One accords with whatever aspect is out of adjustment in proceeding to establish appropriate adjustment of it. One thus brings it about that, throughout the course of a single session of sitting, the three factors of body, respiration, and mind abide in a state of appropriate adjustment. They remain free of any mutual interference and thus become fused in a way whereby there is no longer any dual aspect to them.

此则能除宿患。妨障不生
定道可克。三出时调三事
者。行人若坐禅将竟。欲
出定时。应前放心异缘开
口放气。想从百脉随意而
散。然后微微动身。次动
肩膊及手头颈。次动二足
悉令柔软。次以手遍摩诸
毛孔。次摩手令煖以掩两
眼。然后开之。待身热稍
歇。方可随意出入。若不
尔者坐或得住心。出既顿
促则细法未散住在身中。
令人头痛百骨节彊。犹如
风劳。于后坐中烦躁不
安。是故心欲出定每须在
意。此为出定调身息心方
法。以从细出麁故。是名
善入住出。如偈说

此則能除宿患。妨障不生
定道可剋。三出時調三事
者。行人若坐禪將竟。欲
出定時。應前放心異緣開
口放氣。想從百脈隨意而
散。然後微微動身。次動
肩膊及手頭頸。次動二足
悉令柔軟。次以手遍摩諸
毛孔。次摩手令煖以掩兩
眼。然後開之。待身熱稍
歇。方可隨意出入。若不
爾者坐或得住心。出既頓
促則細法未散住在身中。
令人頭痛百骨節彊。猶如
風勞。於後坐中煩躁不
安。是故心欲出定每須在
意。此為出定調身息心方
法。以從細出麁故。是名
善入住出。如偈說

簡体字　　　　　　　正體字

When this has become the case, one is then able to get rid of any residual disorders rooted in previous existences, one is able to guard against and prevent the arising of obstacles, and one becomes able to establish ascendancy in the path of meditative absorption.

5) [ADJUSTMENTS WHEN EMERGING FROM MEDITATION]

a) [EMERGENCE PROCEDURES]

Third: As for the regulation of the three factors at the time of emerging from meditation, if it is the case that the practitioner's specific session of sitting in dhyāna is about to come to an end, when he wishes to come out of meditative absorption, he should first release his mind onto a different objective condition. Then, he should open his mouth and release the breath while also visualizing it dispersing itself from the many energetic channels in concert with the mental attention.

Afterwards, one should move the body ever so slightly and then move the shoulders and then the hands, the head, and the neck. Next, one moves the two feet and allows them to become entirely limber again. Next, one uses the hands to massage over all of his pores and then massages his hands till they become warm. He then uses them to cover his two eyes and then, afterwards, opens them. Once one has waited for the physical heat to dissipate somewhat, one can then come and go as he pleases.

b) [DANGERS OF NEGLECTING EMERGENCE PROCEDURES]

If one fails to do this, since one may have succeeded in causing the mind to dwell in a particular way during the sit, if one then acts in a sudden and hurried fashion as one comes out of meditation, then the subtle phenomena may not have yet been allowed to disperse. If they thus continue to abide, trapped within the body, they may cause a person to have headaches and to experience a stiffness of all of the joints similar to rheumatism. In subsequent sitting sessions, one may then become afflicted, agitated, and ill at ease. Therefore, when the mind wishes to emerge from meditative absorption, one must always pay careful attention to these points.

This constitutes the technique for regulating the body, respiration, and mind as one emerges from meditative absorption.

6) [CITATIONS RELATING TO ENTRY, ABIDING, EMERGING]

Because one moves forth from the subtle into that which is coarse, this involves a skillful entering, abiding, and emerging as described in a verse:

进止有次第　麁细不相违
譬如善调马　欲住而欲去

[0466c01]　法华经云。此大众诸菩萨等。已于无量千万亿劫。为佛道故勤行精进。善入住出无量百千万亿三昧。得大神通久修梵行。善能次第习诸善法

進止有次第　麁細不相違
譬如善調馬　欲住而欲去

[0466c01]　法華經云。此大眾諸菩薩等。已於無量千萬億劫。為佛道故勤行精進。善入住出無量百千萬億三昧。得大神通久修梵行。善能次第習諸善法

简体字　　　　　　　　　正體字

In moving forward and in stopping, there is a proper sequence.
The coarse and the subtle do not work against each other.
It is just as with the skillful training of a horse.
One wishes to come to a halt and then desires to move along.[6]

In the *Lotus Sutra*, it says: "For the sake of the Buddha Path, the bodhisattvas in this great assembly have already diligently practiced vigor for an incalculable number of tens of millions of *koṭīs* of kalpas. They have become skillful in entering, abiding in, and emerging from an incalculable number of trillions of *koṭīs* of samādhis. They have gained great superknowledges, have long cultivated the brahman conduct, and have become well able to practice in appropriate sequence all of the good dharmas."[7]

## 方便行第五

[0466c06] 夫修止观。须具方便法门。有其五法。一者欲。欲离世间一切妄想颠倒。欲得一切诸禅智慧法门故。亦名为志。亦名为愿。亦名为好。亦名为乐。是人志愿好乐一切诸深法门故。故名为欲。如佛言曰。一切善法欲为其本。二者精进。坚持禁戒弃于五盖。初夜后夜专精不废。譬如钻火未热终不休息。是名精进善道法。三者念念世间为欺诳可贱。念禅定为尊重可贵。若得禅定即能具足。发诸无漏智一切神通道力。成等正觉

简体字

## 方便行第五

[0466c06] 夫修止觀。須具方便法門。有其五法。一者欲。欲離世間一切妄想顛倒。欲得一切諸禪智慧法門故。亦名為志。亦名為願。亦名為好。亦名為樂。是人志願好樂一切諸深法門故。故名為欲。如佛言曰。一切善法欲為其本。二者精進。堅持禁戒棄於五蓋。初夜後夜專精不廢。譬如鑽火未熱終不休息。是名精進善道法。三者念念世間為欺誑可賤。念禪定為尊重可貴。若得禪定即能具足。發諸無漏智一切神通道力。成等正覺

正體字

# CHAPTER FIVE
## Utilizing Skillful Means

5. SECTION FIVE: IMPLEMENTATION OF SKILLFUL MEANS

Now, as for cultivating calming-and-insight, it is necessary to employ various skillful means as entryways into the Dharma. There are five of these dharmas, as follows.

### a. [ZEAL]

The first is zeal (*chanda*). One possesses the zeal to separate from all of the world's erroneous thinking and inverted views. This is because one nurtures the zeal to achieve success in all of the Dharma-access methods associated with dhyāna and wisdom.

This idea may also be referred to by such terms as "being determined to," "aspiring to," "having a fondness for," and "taking pleasure in." This is because such a person is determined towards, aspires to, is fond of, and takes pleasure in all of the profound Dharma-access methods. These are the bases of "zeal." This is as indicated by the Buddha when he said, "Zeal is at the root of all good dharmas."[1]

### b. [VIGOR]

The second is vigor (*vīrya*). One is solid in his observance of the moral prohibitions and in getting rid of the five hindrances. In this, one remains focused and precise, and does not neglect the practice even in the early or later watches of the night. This is analogous to when one employs a friction drill to start a fire. So long as it has not become hot, one must refrain from resting. This is what is meant by vigor as it applies to the good dharmas of the Path.

### c. [MINDFULNESS]

The third is mindfulness (*smṛti*). One remains continuously mindful that the world is deceptive and deserves to be deemed base whereas dhyāna absorption is honorable and worthy to be regarded as noble. If one gains dhyāna absorption, one immediately becomes able to perfectly generate the wisdom free of outflow-impurities, all of the superknowledges, the aspects of the Path, and the powers. One becomes able to achieve the equal and right enlightenment

广度众生。是为可贵。故名为念。四者巧慧。筹量世间乐。禅定智慧乐得失轻重。所以者何。世间之乐。乐少苦多虚诳不实。是失是轻。禅定智慧之乐。无漏无为寂然闲旷。永离生死。与苦长别是得是重。如是分别故名巧慧。五者一心。分明明见世间可患可恶。善识定慧功德可尊可贵。尔时应当一心决定修行止观。心如金刚天魔外道不能沮坏。设使空无所获终不回易。是名一心。譬如人行先须知道通塞之相。然后决定一心涉路而进。故说巧慧一心。经云。非智不禅非禅不智。义在此也

廣度眾生。是為可貴。故名為念。四者巧慧。籌量世間樂。禪定智慧樂得失輕重。所以者何。世間之樂。樂少苦多虛誑不實。是失是輕。禪定智慧之樂。無漏無為寂然閑曠。永離生死。與苦長別是得是重。如是分別故名巧慧。五者一心。分明明見世間可患可惡。善識定慧功德可尊可貴。爾時應當一心決定修行止觀。心如金剛天魔外道不能沮壞。設使空無所獲終不回易。是名一心。譬如人行先須知道通塞之相。然後決定一心涉路而進。故說巧慧一心。經云。非智不禪非禪不智。義在此也

简体字                                                          正體字

and to engage extensively in the spiritual liberation of beings. This is worthy of being regarded as noble. These considerations define what is meant here by "mindfulness."

d. [DISCERNMENT]

The fourth is discernment (*samprajñāna*). One makes a critical comparison between worldly happiness and the happiness associated with dhyāna absorption and wisdom, judging the achievements against the losses and the worthless against the valuable. How so? As for the happiness of the world, the happiness is but little, whereas its suffering is extensive. It is false, deceptive, and unreal. This amounts to a loss and to involvement in what is worthless.

As for the happiness which accompanies dhyāna absorption and wisdom, it is free of outflow-impurities, unconditioned, serene, and carefree. One eternally transcends cyclic births and deaths and remains forever free from suffering. This amounts to an achievement and to the realization of what is valuable. Analyses such as these form the basis of discernment.

e. [SINGLE-MINDEDNESS]

The fifth is the practice of single-mindedness (*citta-eka-agra*). Through making clear distinctions, one perceives with clarity that it is fitting to regard the world as vexing and loathsome. One recognizes well that the meritorious qualities of meditative absorption and wisdom are worthy to be deemed honorable and noble. At such a time, one should make a single-minded decision to cultivate calming-and insight, making one's mind like *vajra* so that the heavenly demons and the non-Buddhists will be unable to interfere with or destroy [one's practice]. One's determination should be such that, even if one's efforts come up empty and nothing whatsoever is gained, one will still persevere to the end and not turn back or change one's resolve. This is what is meant by single-mindedness.

This [utilization of five skillful-means dharmas] is analogous to [essential factors involved in] a person's travels. It is first necessary to know the signs of the open or obstructed road. Afterwards, one decides to proceed single-mindedly along the road and then advances accordingly. Hence we speak here of discernment and single-mindedness. One of the sutras states, "Were it not for wisdom, one would not course in dhyāna. Were it not for dhyāna, one would not exercise wisdom."[2] This is the essential idea here.

| 正修行第六 | 正修行第六 |
|---|---|
| [0466c28] 修止观者有二种。一者于坐中修。二者历缘对境修。一于坐中修止观者。于四威仪中亦乃皆得。然学道者坐为胜故。先约坐以明止观。略出五意不同。一对治初心麁乱修止观。所谓行者初坐禅时心麁乱故。应当修止以除破之。止若不破即应修观。故云对破初心麁乱修止观。 | [0466c28] 修止觀者有二種。一者於坐中修。二者歷緣對境修。一於坐中修止觀者。於四威儀中亦乃皆得。然學道者坐為勝故。先約坐以明止觀。略出五意不同。一對治初心麁亂修止觀。所謂行者初坐禪時心麁亂故。應當修止以除破之。止若不破即應修觀。故云對破初心麁亂修止觀。 |

简体字                                正體字

# CHAPTER SIX

## The Actual Cultivation

6. SECTION SIX: THE ACTUAL CULTIVATION

As for the cultivation of calming-and-insight, there are two modes. The first is cultivation while sitting. The second is cultivation while moving through objective conditions and as one relates to the objective sphere.

### a. [CALMING-AND-INSIGHT DURING SITTING MEDITATION]

As for the first mode, the cultivation as one cultivates calming-and-insight while sitting, although it is true that this can be accomplished in any of the four deportments,[1] still, for the study of the path, sitting is the superior posture. Therefore one first explains calming-and-insight in relation to sitting. Generally speaking, one sets forth five different concepts in this connection:

[1] Cultivating calming-and-insight as means of countering the coarseness and disorderedness of the beginner's mind;

2) Cultivating calming-and-insight as means of countering the faults of mental "sinking," or "floating";

3) Cultivating calming-and-insight in a manner which accords with whatever is appropriate;

4) Cultivating calming-and-insight to counteract subtle states of mind occurring in meditative absorption;

5) Cultivating calming-and-insight as means of achieving equal balance in meditative absorption and wisdom.[2]

### 1) [CALMING-AND-INSIGHT COUNTERING MENTAL COARSENESS & DISORDEREDNESS]

The first concept is cultivating calming-and-insight as means of countering the coarseness and disorderedness of the beginner's mind. This refers to the case where, because the practitioner's thoughts are coarse and disordered when he first attempts to sit in dhyāna, he should then cultivate calming to get rid of them and break their hold. If one is unable to break their hold through calming, then one ought in such a case to cultivate insight. Hence one speaks of cultivating calming-and-insight in order to counter and break the coarseness and disorderedness of the beginner's mind.

今明修止观有二意。一者
修止自有三种。一者系缘
守境止。所谓系心鼻端脐
间等处。令心不散。故经
云。系心不放逸亦如猿着
锁。二者制心止所谓随心
所起即便制之不令驰散。
故经云。此五根者心为其
主。是故汝等当好止心。
此二种皆是事相不须分
别。三者体真止。所谓随
心所念。一切诸法悉知从
因缘生。无有自性。则心
不取。若心不取则妄念心
息。故名为止。如经中说
云

一切诸法中　因缘空无主
息心达本源　故号为沙门

[0467a16] 行者于初坐禅时。
随心所念一切诸法。念念
不住。虽用如上体真止而
妄念不息。当反观所起之
心。

今明修止觀有二意。一者
修止自有三種。一者繫緣
守境止。所謂繫心鼻端臍
間等處。令心不散。故經
云。繫心不放逸亦如猿著
鎖。二者制心止所謂隨心
所起即便制之不令馳散。
故經云。此五根者心為其
主。是故汝等當好止心。
此二種皆是事相不須分
別。三者體真止。所謂隨
心所念。一切諸法悉知從
因緣生。無有自性。則心
不取。若心不取則妄念心
息。故名為止。如經中說
云

一切諸法中　因緣空無主
息心達本源　故號為沙門

[0467a16] 行者於初坐禪時。
隨心所念一切諸法。念念
不住。雖用如上體真止而
妄念不息。當反觀所起之
心。

简体字　　　　　　　　　　正體字

a) [CALMING DURING SITTING MEDITATION]

Now, the explanation of the cultivation of calming-and-insight involves two concepts. The first, the cultivation of calming, involves the use of three methods:

i) [CALMING BY ANCHORING ATTENTION ON AN OBJECT IN THE OBJECTIVE SPHERE]

The first of these is calming wherein one anchors one's attention on a particular condition while monitoring the objective sphere. This refers to anchoring the mind at such locations as the tip of the nose or the navel in order to prevent the mind from becoming scattered. Accordingly, a sutra states, "One anchors the mind and refrains from falling into neglectfulness. This is just like locking up a monkey."[3]

ii) [CALMING THROUGH CONTROLLING THE MIND]

The second is calming through controlling the mind. This refers to exerting control no matter what comes up in the mind in order to prevent it from running off and becoming scattered. A sutra says, "As for these five sense faculties, the mind acts as their ruler. Therefore, you should all skillfully control your minds."[4]

Because both of these approaches are characterized by [obvious] phenomena, it is not necessary to analyze them here.

iii) [CALMING THROUGH REALIZATION OF TRUTH]

The third is calming through realization of truth. This means that, no matter what the mind dwells upon, if one understands that all dharmas are produced from causes and conditions and are devoid of an inherently-existent nature, then the mind will not seize upon them. If the mind does not seize upon them, then the false-thinking mind will come to a rest. Hence this qualifies as calming. This is as described in a sutra where it states:

As for each and every one of all the dharmas,
Consisting of causes and conditions, they are empty, devoid of
    any [inherently-existent] entity.
One puts the mind to rest and penetrates to the original source.
It is on this account that one is known as a "śramaṇa."[5]

When the practitioner first sits in dhyāna meditation, [he observes that], no matter what the mind thinks of, no dharma abides for even an instant. If one's false thoughts do not cease even though one has implemented the above-described technique of calming through realization of truth, one should then reflect upon the mind which

过去已灭。现在不住。未来未至。三际穷之了不可得。不可得法则无有心。若无有心则一切法皆无。行者虽观心不住皆无所有。而非无刹那。任运觉知念起。又观此心念以内有六根外有六尘。根尘相对故有识生。根尘未对识本无生。观生如是观灭亦然。生灭名字但是假立。生灭心灭。寂灭现前了无所得。是所谓涅盘空寂之理。其心自止。起信论云。若心驰散即当摄来住于正念。是正念者当知唯心无外境界。即复此心亦无自相。念念不可得谓初心修学未便得住。抑之令住往往发狂。如学射法久习方中矣。

過去已滅。現在不住。未來未至。三際窮之了不可得。不可得法則無有心。若無有心則一切法皆無。行者雖觀心不住皆無所有。而非無刹那。任運覺知念起。又觀此心念以內有六根外有六塵。根塵相對故有識生。根塵未對識本無生。觀生如是觀滅亦然。生滅名字但是假立。生滅心滅。寂滅現前了無所得。是所謂涅槃空寂之理。其心自止。起信論云。若心馳散即當攝來住於正念。是正念者當知唯心無外境界。即復此心亦無自相。念念不可得謂初心修學未便得住。抑之令住往往發狂。如學射法久習方中矣。

简体字                                    正體字

gives rise [to these thoughts], and realize that, as for the past, that has already been destroyed, as for the present, it does not abide, and as for the future, it has not yet come. When one searches throughout these three periods of time, it cannot be found at all. If it constitutes a dharma which cannot be found, then there is no [inherently existent] mind. If there is no such [inherently existent] mind, then all dharmas are themselves devoid of any [inherent] existence.

Although the practitioner contemplates and finds that the mind does not abide and is in every case devoid of any [inherent] existence, still, it is not the case that there is no *kṣaṇa-after-kṣaṇa*[6] (millisecond-level) process wherein one carries forth with the generation of an aware and knowing mindfulness.

One additionally contemplates this mind's thought, observing that it is on account of the inward presence of the six sense faculties, the outward presence of the six sense objects, and the mutual opposition between the faculties and the objects that one thereby generates consciousness. When the sense faculties and the sense objects have not yet been placed in mutual opposition, there is fundamentally no production of [any corresponding sense] consciousness. Just as one contemplates the process of production in this manner, so too does one contemplate the process of cessation in precisely the same way.

The names "production" and "cessation" are only falsely established. When the mind characterized by production and cessation ceases, then quiescent cessation manifests right before one. There is then nothing whatsoever therein which can be found to exist. This is the so-called empty and still noumenal principle of nirvāṇa. One's mind then naturally comes to a halt, [achieving a state of "calming."]

The *Awakening of Faith Treatise* states, "If the mind has run off and become scattered, one should immediately draw it back in and establish it in right mindfulness. As for this 'right mindfulness,' one should be aware that it is only mind. There is no outward realm. This very mind itself is devoid of any inherently existent characteristic. Even from one instant to the next, its existence cannot be found."[7]

It is said that there are beginners in the cultivation of this study who, not yet having developed an easy ability to still the mind, attempt to suppress it to force it to remain still. [Those adopting such an approach] often become prone to mental derangement.

二者修观有二种。一者对
治观。如不净观对治贪
欲。慈心观对治瞋恚。界
分别观对治着我数息观对
治多寻思等。此不分别
也。二者正观。观诸法无
相并是因缘所生。因缘无
性即是实相。先了所观之
境一切皆空。能观之心自
然不起。前后之文多谈此
理。请自详之。如经偈中
说

诸法不牢固　常在于念中
已解见空者　一切无想念

[0467b10] 　二对治心沈浮病
修止观。行者于坐禅时。
其心暗塞无记瞪瞢。或时
多睡。尔时应当修观照
了。若于坐中其心浮动轻
躁不安。尔时应当修止止
之。

二者修觀有二種。一者對
治觀。如不淨觀對治貪
欲。慈心觀對治瞋恚。界
分別觀對治著我數息觀對
治多尋思等。此不分別
也。二者正觀。觀諸法無
相並是因緣所生。因緣無
性即是實相。先了所觀之
境一切皆空。能觀之心自
然不起。前後之文多談此
理。請自詳之。如經偈中
說

諸法不牢固　常在於念中
已解見空者　一切無想念

[0467b10] 　二對治心沈浮病
修止觀。行者於坐禪時。
其心闇塞無記瞪瞢。或時
多睡。爾時應當修觀照
了。若於坐中其心浮動輕
躁不安。爾時應當修止止
之。

简体字　　　　正體字

This is just like studying archery. If one were to devote a long time to the practice, one would succeed in hitting the bulls-eye.

b) [Insight During Sitting Meditation]

The second, the cultivation of insight, is of two types.

i) [Counteractive Insight]

The first is counteractive insight. It is exemplified by the contemplation of impurity aimed at counteracting desire, the contemplation involving the mind of loving-kindness aimed at counteracting hatred, the contemplation involving analysis of the sense realms aimed at counteracting attachment to a self, and the breath-counting contemplation aimed at counteracting excessive discursive thinking. These will not be discussed in detail here.

ii) [Right (Insight) Contemplation]

The second, right [insight] contemplation, involves the contemplation of all dharmas as devoid of [inherently existent] aspects and also as produced from causes and conditions. The absence of an [inherently-existent] nature owing to [being reducible to mere] causes and conditions is itself their true character.[8] If one first comprehends that absolutely everything within the contemplated sphere is entirely empty [of any inherent existence], then the mind capable of engaging in contemplation naturally does not arise.

The earlier and later parts of the text devote considerable attention to discussing this concept. The reader is requested to study this in detail himself. The concept is illustrated by a sutra verse which states:

All dharmas are insubstantial.
They constantly abide in one's thoughts.
One who has understood and perceived emptiness
Is in every case free of thinking.[9]

2) [Calming-and-Insight Countering Mental "Sinking" or "Floating"]

The second concept involves cultivating calming-and-insight as means of countering the faults of mental "sinking," or "floating."

When the practitioner is sitting in dhyāna meditation, if his mind is obstructed by dimness and fails to attend to anything as he stares blankly, or if he becomes prone at times to much sleepiness, he should then cultivate insight to bring forth illumination.

是则略说对治心沈浮病修
止观相。但须善识药病相
对用之。一一不得于对治
有乖僻之失。三随便宜修
止观。行者于坐禅时。虽
为对治心沈故修于观照。
而心不明净亦无法利。尔
时当试修止止之。若于止
时即觉身心安静。当知宜
止。即应用止安心。若于
坐禅时。虽为对治心浮动
故修止。而心不住。亦无
法利。当试修观。若于观
中。即觉心神明净寂然安
隐。当知宜观。即当用观
安心。是则略说随便宜修
止观相。但须善约便宜修
之则心神安隐烦恼患息。
证诸法门也。四对治定中
细心修止观。所谓行者先
用止观对破麁乱。

是則略說對治心沈浮病修
止觀相。但須善識藥病相
對用之。一一不得於對治
有乖僻之失。三隨便宜修
止觀。行者於坐禪時。雖
為對治心沈故修於觀照。
而心不明淨亦無法利。爾
時當試修止止之。若於止
時即覺身心安靜。當知宜
止。即應用止安心。若於
坐禪時。雖為對治心浮動
故修止。而心不住。亦無
法利。當試修觀。若於觀
中。即覺心神明淨寂然安
隱。當知宜觀。即當用觀
安心。是則略說隨便宜修
止觀相。但須善約便宜修
之則心神安隱煩惱患息。
證諸法門也。四對治定中
細心修止觀。所謂行者先
用止觀對破麁亂。

簡体字 　　　　　　　 正體字

If, in the midst of sitting, one's mind moves about in a floating manner such that it is light, agitated, and ill at ease, one should then cultivate calming in order to bring it to a halt.

This is a summary explanation of the features of cultivating calming-and-insight as means of countering the faults of mental "sinking," or "floating." It is only necessary that in utilizing them, one understands well how to match the medicine and the disorder. One must refrain in every case from committing the error of applying the antidotes in a contrary or unorthodox manner.

### 3) [CALMING-AND-INSIGHT IN ACCORDANCE WITH WHATEVER IS APPROPRIATE]

The third concept involves cultivating calming-and-insight in a manner according with whatever is appropriate.

When the practitioner is sitting in dhyāna meditation, if, even though he does cultivate contemplative illumination for the sake of counteracting mental sinking, his mind still does not become bright and pure and there is no Dharma-related benefit from it, he should then try cultivating calming in order to arrest it. If, when he is utilizing calming, he then becomes aware of his body and mind having become peaceful and still, he should know then that it is appropriate to utilize calming. He should then employ calming to pacify the mind.

When one is sitting in dhyāna meditation, if, even though he cultivates calming to counteract mental floating and moving about, the mind still does not come to a stop and he derives no Dharma-related benefit from it, he should then try cultivating [insight] contemplation. If, in the midst of [insight] contemplation, he then becomes aware that the mind and spirit have become bright, pure, still, and stable, he ought to know then that it is appropriate to engage in [insight] contemplation. He should then employ [insight] contemplation to pacify the mind.

This is a summary explanation of the features of cultivating calming-and-insight in a manner which accords with whatever is appropriate. It is only necessary that one skillfully adapt to what is appropriate and cultivate that. If one does this, then the mind and spirit will become peaceful and stable, the calamity of the afflictions will be put to rest, and one will realize success in cultivating entryways to Dharma.

### 4) [CALMING-AND-INSIGHT COUNTERING SUBTLE MIND STATES]

The fourth concept involves cultivating calming-and-insight to

乱心既息即得入定。定心
细故觉身空寂受于快乐。
或利便心发能以细心取于
偏邪之理。若不知定心止
息虚诳。必生贪着。若生
贪着执以为实。若知虚诳
不实。即爱见二烦恼不
起。是为修止。虽复修止
若心犹着爱见结业不息。
尔时应当修观。观于定中
细心。若不见定中细心。
即不执着定见。若不执着
定见。则爱见烦恼业悉皆
摧灭。是名修观。此则略
说对治定中细心修止观
相。分别止观方法并同于
前。但以破定见微细之失
为异也。五为均齐定慧修
止观。行者于坐禅中因修
止故。或因修观而入禅
定。

亂心既息即得入定。定心
細故覺身空寂受於快樂。
或利便心發能以細心取於
偏邪之理。若不知定心止
息虛誑。必生貪著。若生
貪著執以為實。若知虛誑
不實。即愛見二煩惱不
起。是為修止。雖復修止
若心猶著愛見結業不息。
爾時應當修觀。觀於定中
細心。若不見定中細心。
即不執著定見。若不執著
定見。則愛見煩惱業悉皆
摧滅。是名修觀。此則略
說對治定中細心修止觀
相。分別止觀方法並同於
前。但以破定見微細之失
為異也。五為均齊定慧修
止觀。行者於坐禪中因修
止故。或因修觀而入禪
定。

简体字　　　　　　正體字

counteract subtle states of mind occurring in meditative absorption. This refers to the situation where the practitioner has first utilized calming-and-insight to counteract and break the hold of coarse and disordered states and, because the disordered thought has already ceased, he then succeeds in entering meditative absorption.

On account of the subtle mind state arising in meditative absorption, one becomes aware of the body as empty and still and then experiences bliss. It may be that a mind prone to indulgence is then brought forth which is able to use that subtle mental state as a basis for seizing on deviant ideas.

If one remains unaware of the false and deceptive nature of the mind which has come to a rest in meditative absorption, one will certainly become desirously attached to this experience. If one becomes desirously attached, one will cling to this as being genuine. If, however, one is aware that this is false, deceptive, and not genuine, then the two afflictions of affection and views will not arise. This then would constitute the cultivation of calming.

If, even though one continues to cultivate calming, the mind still remains attached and the karma of the fetters linked to affection and views does not cease, one should then cultivate [insight] contemplation, directing that contemplation to the subtle mind involved in meditative absorption.

If one does not then perceive [any inherent existence of] those subtle mind states arising in meditative absorption, then one will not retain any attachment to the [wrong] views associated with this meditative absorption. If one does not establish attachment to those [wrong] views associated with this meditative absorption, then the karma associated with the afflictions of affection and views will all be entirely shattered and destroyed. This then would constitute the cultivation of [insight] contemplation.

This is a summary explanation of the features of cultivating calming-and-insight to counteract the subtle mental states occurring in meditative absorption. The distinguishing features associated with the methods of calming-and-insight are identical to those set forth previously. The only difference in this case is that they are employed here to demolish especially subtle errors inherent in [particular] views associated with meditative absorption.

    5) [CALMING-AND-INSIGHT TO ACHIEVE BALANCE IN ABSORPTION AND WISDOM]

The fifth concept is the cultivation of calming-and-insight as means of achieving equal balance in meditative absorption and wisdom.

虽得入定而无观慧。是为痴定。不能断结。或观慧微少。即不能发起真慧。断诸结使发诸法门。尔时应当修观破析则定慧均等。能断结使证诸法门。行者于坐禅时。因修观故而心豁然开悟。智慧分明而定心微少。心则动散。如风中灯照物不了。不能出离生死。尔时应当复修于止。以修止故则得定心。如密室中灯则能破暗照物分明。是则略说均齐定慧二法修止观也。行者若能如是于端身正坐之中。善用此五番修止观意。取舍不失其宜。当知是人善修佛法。能善修故必于一。生不空过也。复次第二明历缘对境修止观者。

雖得入定而無觀慧。是為癡定。不能斷結。或觀慧微少。即不能發起真慧。斷諸結使發諸法門。爾時應當修觀破析則定慧均等。能斷結使證諸法門。行者於坐禪時。因修觀故而心豁然開悟。智慧分明而定心微少。心則動散。如風中燈照物不了。不能出離生死。爾時應當復修於止。以修止故則得定心。如密室中燈則能破暗照物分明。是則略說均齊定慧二法修止觀也。行者若能如是於端身正坐之中。善用此五番修止觀意。取捨不失其宜。當知是人善修佛法。能善修故必於一。生不空過也。復次第二明歷緣對境修止觀者。

简体字　　　　正體字

While sitting in dhyāna, either on account of cultivating calming or perhaps on account of cultivating [insight] contemplation, the practitioner may then enter dhyāna absorption. Having done so, although he may have succeeded in entering meditative absorption, still, he may not possess any [insight] contemplation-based wisdom. This constitutes an absorption characterized by stupidity, one wherein one remains unable to cut off the fetters. Or it might also happen that the operative [insight] contemplation-based wisdom is only faint and scant. In such a case, one is unable to generate true wisdom, sever the fetters, or develop the entryways to Dharma.

At such a time, one should cultivate the analysis of [insight] contemplation. If one does so, then meditative absorption and wisdom become equally balanced, one becomes able to sever the fetters, and one achieves realization in the entryways to Dharma.

When the practitioner is sitting in dhyāna, on account of cultivating [insight] contemplation, his mind may suddenly open up and become awakened such that his wisdom becomes sharp and clear. However, it may be that the mind of meditative absorption is still only faint and scant. In such a case, the mind may become subject to moving and scattering. Then, just like a lamp flame in the wind, it cannot completely illuminate things. In such a case, one remains unable to succeed in abandoning cyclic births and deaths.

At such a time, one should return to the cultivation of calming. On account of cultivating calming, one then gains the mind of meditative absorption. Then, like the lamp flame which burns in a closed room, it becomes immediately able to dispel the darkness and illuminate things clearly.

This is a summary explanation of the cultivation of the two dharmas of calming and insight in order to establish equal balance of meditative absorption and wisdom.

6) [Benefits of Skillful Utilization of the Five Concepts]

If the practitioner is able in this manner to skillfully utilize these five ideas in cultivating calming-and-insight in sitting meditation, and if he does not fail to accord with what is appropriate in selecting them and dispensing with them, then one should realize that this person skillfully cultivates the Dharma of the Buddha. Because one is able to skillfully cultivate them, he most certainly will not pass through this one lifetime in vain.

b. [Objective Sphere Related Calming-and-Insight]

端身常坐乃为入道之胜
要。而有累之身必涉事
缘。若随缘对境而不修习
止观。是则修心有间绝。
结业触处而起。岂得疾与
佛法相应。若于一切时
中。常修定慧方便。当知
是人必能通达一切佛法。
云何名历缘修止观。所言
缘者。谓六种缘。一行二
住三坐四卧五作作(下祖
卧切)六言语。云何名对
境修止观。所言境者谓六
尘境。一眼对色。二耳对
声。三鼻对香。四舌对
味。五身对触。六意对
法。行者约此十二事中。
修止观故名为历缘对境修
止观也。一行者若于行时
应作是念。我今为何等事
欲行。为烦恼所使。及不
善无记事行即不应行。若
非烦恼所使。为善利益如
法事即应行。

端身常坐乃為入道之勝
要。而有累之身必涉事
緣。若隨緣對境而不修習
止觀。是則修心有間絕。
結業觸處而起。豈得疾與
佛法相應。若於一切時
中。常修定慧方便。當知
是人必能通達一切佛法。
云何名歷緣修止觀。所言
緣者。謂六種緣。一行二
住三坐四臥五作作(下祖
臥切)六言語。云何名對
境修止觀。所言境者謂六
塵境。一眼對色。二耳對
聲。三鼻對香。四舌對
味。五身對觸。六意對
法。行者約此十二事中。
修止觀故名為歷緣對境修
止觀也。一行者若於行時
應作是念。我今為何等事
欲行。為煩惱所使。及不
善無記事行即不應行。若
非煩惱所使。為善利益如
法事即應行。

简体字　　　　　　　　　　　正體字

Next, the second mode. Here we explain the cultivation of calming-and-insight while moving through objective conditions and while relating to the objective sphere.

Constantly sitting with the body upright is the supreme essential for entering the Path. However, a person with responsibilities must necessarily be involved in conditions related to his endeavors. If one adapts to objective conditions in relating to the objective sphere and yet fails to cultivate calming-and-insight, this will produce interruptions in his cultivation of the mind. In such a case, the karma of the fetters will arise at any point of contact. In such a case, how could one succeed in achieving a rapid conformity with the Dharma of the Buddha?

If a person is at all times constantly cultivating skillful means related to meditative absorption and wisdom, one should know that this person will certainly be able to reach a penetrating understanding of all of the Buddha's dharmas.

What is meant by cultivating calming-and-insight as one moves through objective conditions? As for what is referred to as "objective conditions," it refers to six kinds of objective conditions: The first is walking; the second is standing; the third is sitting; the fourth is lying down; the fifth is doing things; and the sixth is speaking.

What is meant by cultivating calming-and-insight while relating to the objective sphere? As for what is referred to as "the objective sphere," it refers to the sphere of the six sense objects: The first is the eye in relation to forms; the second is the ear in relation to sounds; the third is the nose in relation to fragrances; the fourth is the tongue in relation to flavors; the fifth is the body in relation to tangibles; and the sixth is the intellectual mind in relation to dharmas [as objects of mind].

It is based on the practitioner's cultivation of calming-and-insight in relation to these twelve phenomena that one speaks of the cultivation of calming-and-insight as one moves through objective conditions and as one relates to the objective sphere.

1) [When Moving Through Six Karmic Modes]

a) [When Walking]

First, walking. At times when one is involved in walking, one should bring forth this thought: "For what purpose do I now wish to walk?" If it is on account of being directed by afflictions or by unwholesome or neutral matters, then one should not proceed with walking. If it is not an instance of being directed by the afflictions

云何行中修止。若于行时
即知因于行故。则有一切
烦恼善恶等法。了知行心
及行中一切法皆不可得。
则妄念心息。是名修止。
云何行中修观。应作是
念。由心动身。故有进
趣。名之为行。因此行
故。则有一切烦恼善恶等
法。即当反观行心不见相
貌。当知行者及行中。一
切法毕竟空寂。是名修
观。二住者。若于住时应
作是念。我今为何等事欲
住。若为诸烦恼及不善无
记事住。即不应住。若为
善利益事即应住。云何住
中修止。若于住时即知因
于住故。则有一切烦恼善
恶等法。了知住心及住中
一切法。皆不可得。则妄
念心息。是名修止。云何
住中修观。应作是念。由

簡体字

云何行中修止。若於行時
即知因於行故。則有一切
煩惱善惡等法。了知行心
及行中一切法皆不可得。
則妄念心息。是名修止。
云何行中修觀。應作是
念。由心動身。故有進
趣。名之為行。因此行
故。則有一切煩惱善惡等
法。即當反觀行心不見相
貌。當知行者及行中。一
切法畢竟空寂。是名修
觀。二住者。若於住時應
作是念。我今為何等事欲
住。若為諸煩惱及不善無
記事住。即不應住。若為
善利益事即應住。云何住
中修止。若於住時即知因
於住故。則有一切煩惱善
惡等法。了知住心及住中
一切法。皆不可得。則妄
念心息。是名修止。云何
住中修觀。應作是念。由

正體字

and if it is for the sake of a matter which produces wholesome benefits and which is in accord with the Dharma, then one should go ahead and proceed with walking.

### i) [CALMING WHEN WALKING]

How does one go about cultivating calming while walking? If one is walking, one maintains the awareness that, on account of walking, there may then come to exist all of the dharmas of the afflictions, of good, of bad, and so forth. If one is completely aware that the mind engaged in walking as well as all dharmas present in walking cannot be found, then the false-thinking mind ceases. It is this which constitutes the cultivation of calming.

### ii) [INSIGHT WHEN WALKING]

How does one go about cultivating [insight] contemplation while walking? One should bring forth this thought: "It is on account of the mind that one moves the body. As a result, one brings about that forward movement referred to as 'walking.' It is on account of walking that there may then come to exist all of the dharmas of the afflictions, of good, of bad, and so forth."

One should then immediately turn back the attention and contemplate the mind which is engaged in walking. One then fails to perceive any characteristic appearance associated with it. One should then realize that the one who walks as well as all dharmas involved in walking are both ultimately empty and still. It is this which constitutes the cultivation of [insight] contemplation.

### b) [WHEN STANDING]

Second, standing. If one is standing, one should bring forth this thought: "On account of what endeavor do I now wish to stand?" If it is for the sake of the afflictions or unwholesome or neutral endeavors that one proposes to stand, then one should not proceed with standing. If it is for the sake of good and beneficial endeavors, then one should engage in standing.

### i) [CALMING WHEN STANDING]

How does one cultivate calming while standing? If one is standing, one maintains the awareness that, on account of standing, there may then come to exist all of the dharmas of the afflictions, of good, of bad, and so forth. If one is completely aware that the mind engaged in standing as well as all of the dharmas involved in standing cannot be found, then the false-thinking mind comes to rest. It is this which constitutes the cultivation of calming.

心驻身故名为住。因此住故则有一切烦恼善恶等法。则当反观住心。不见相貌。当知住者及住中一切法毕竟空寂。是名修观。三坐者。若于坐时应作是念。我今为何等事欲坐。若为诸烦恼及不善无记事等。即不应坐。为善利益事则应坐。云何坐中修止。若于坐时则当了知因于坐故。则有一切烦恼。善恶等法。而无一法可得。则妄念不生。是名修止。云何坐中修观。应作是念。由心所念垒脚安身。因此则有一切善恶等法故名为坐。反观坐心不见相貌。当知坐者及坐中。一切法毕竟空寂。是名修观四卧者。于卧时应作是念。我今为何等事欲

心駐身故名為住。因此住故則有一切煩惱善惡等法。則當反觀住心。不見相貌。當知住者及住中一切法畢竟空寂。是名修觀。三坐者。若於坐時應作是念。我今為何等事欲坐。若為諸煩惱及不善無記事等。即不應坐。為善利益事則應坐。云何坐中修止。若於坐時則當了知因於坐故。則有一切煩惱。善惡等法。而無一法可得。則妄念不生。是名修止。云何坐中修觀。應作是念。由心所念疊腳安身。因此則有一切善惡等法故名為坐。反觀坐心不見相貌。當知坐者及坐中。一切法畢竟空寂。是名修觀四臥者。於臥時應作是念。我今為何等事欲

简体字　　　　正體字

ii) [INSIGHT WHEN STANDING]

How does one go about cultivating [insight] contemplation while standing? One should bring forth this thought: "It is on account of the mind that the body is brought to a stop. As a result, one refers to 'standing.' It is on account of this standing that there may then exist all of the dharmas of the afflictions, of good, of bad, and so forth."

One should then turn back one's attention and contemplate the mind engaged in standing. One then fails to perceive any characteristic appearance in it. One should then realize that the one who stands as well as all of the dharmas involved in standing are ultimately empty and still. It is this which constitutes the cultivation of [insight] contemplation.

c) [WHEN SITTING]

Third, sitting. If one is sitting, one should bring forth this thought: "On account of what endeavor do I now wish to sit?" If it is to indulge the afflictions or for the sake of unwholesome or neutral matters, then one should not proceed to sit. If it is for the sake of good and beneficial endeavors, then one should proceed with sitting.

i) [CALMING WHEN SITTING]

How does one go about cultivating calming while sitting? If one is engaged in sitting, then one should be completely aware that, on account of sitting, there may then come to exist all of the dharmas of the afflictions, of good, of bad, and so forth. However, if [one remains aware that] there is not one single dharma which can be found, then false thoughts will not arise. It is this which constitutes the cultivation of calming.

ii) [INSIGHT WHEN SITTING]

How does one go about cultivating [insight] contemplation while sitting? One should bring forth this thought: "It is on account of what is thought by the mind that one stabilizes the body in the cross-legged posture. It is on account of this that one may come to have all of the dharmas of good, of bad, and so forth. Thus it is that one refers to 'sitting.'"

In turning around the attention to contemplate the mind engaged in sitting, one does not perceive any characteristic appearance. One should then realize that the one who sits as well as all of the dharmas involved in sitting are ultimately empty and still. It is this which constitutes the cultivation of [insight] contemplation.

卧若为不善放逸等事。则不应卧。若为调和四大故卧。则应如师子王卧。云何卧中修止。若于寝息则当了知因于卧故。则有一切善恶等法。而无一法可得则妄念不起。是名修止。云何卧中修观。应作是念。由于劳乏即便昏暗放纵六情。因此则有一切烦恼。善恶等法。即当反观卧心不见相貌。当知卧者及卧中。一切法毕竟空寂。是名修观。五作者。若作时应作是念。我今为何等事欲如此作。若为不善无记等事。即不应作。若为善利益事即应作。云何名作中修止。若于作时即当了知。因于作故则有一切善恶等法。而无一法

卧若為不善放逸等事。則不應臥。若為調和四大故臥。則應如師子王臥。云何臥中修止。若於寢息則當了知因於臥故。則有一切善惡等法。而無一法可得則妄念不起。是名修止。云何臥中修觀。應作是念。由於勞乏即便昏闇放縱六情。因此則有一切煩惱。善惡等法。即當反觀臥心不見相貌。當知臥者及臥中。一切法畢竟空寂。是名修觀。五作者。若作時應作是念。我今為何等事欲如此作。若為不善無記等事。即不應作。若為善利益事即應作。云何名作中修止。若於作時即當了知。因於作故則有一切善惡等法。而無一法

简体字　　　　　　正體字

d) [WHEN LYING DOWN]

Fourth, lying down. When one is lying down, one should bring forth this thought: "On account of what endeavor do I now wish to lie down?" If it is on account of some matter which is unwholesome or neglectful, then one should not proceed with lying down. If it is for the sake of bringing the four great elements into adjustment and harmony, then one ought to proceed with lying down like the King of Lions.[10]

i) [CALMING WHEN LYING DOWN]

How does one go about cultivating calming when lying down? If one is going to sleep, then one ought to become completely aware that, on account of lying down, there may come to exist all manner of dharmas of good, of bad, and so forth. However, if [one remains aware that] there is not one single dharma which can be found, then false thinking will not arise. It is this which constitutes the cultivation of calming.

ii) [INSIGHT WHEN LYING DOWN]

How does one go about cultivating [insight] contemplation when lying down? One should bring forth this thought: "It is on account of becoming worn out and exhausted that one then becomes beclouded and dim and then lets loose of the six sense faculties. It is on account of this that there may then come to exist all of the dharmas of the afflictions, of good, of bad, and so forth."

One should then turn back one's attention and contemplate the mind involved in lying down. One fails to perceive any characteristic appearance in it. One should then realize that the one who lies down as well as all of the dharmas involved in lying down are ultimately empty and still. It is this which constitutes the cultivation of [insight] contemplation.

e) [WHEN ENGAGING IN ACTIONS]

Fifth, engaging in actions. When one is engaging in actions, one should bring forth this thought: "On account of what matter do I now wish to engage in an action such as this?" If it is for the sake of matters which are unwholesome, neutral, and so forth, then one should not proceed to act. If it is for the sake of good and beneficial matters, then one should proceed with the action.

i) [CALMING WHEN ENGAGING IN ACTIONS]

How does one go about cultivating calming in the midst of engaging in actions? If one is involved in carrying out actions, then one

可得则妄念不起。是名修
止。云何名作时修观。应
作是念。由心运于身。手
造作诸事。因此则有一切
善恶等法故名为作。反观
作心不见相貌。当知作者
及作中一切法毕竟空寂。
是名修观。六语者。若于
语时应作是念。我今为何
等事欲语。若随诸烦恼。
为论说不善无记等事而
语。即不应语。若为善利
益事即应语。云何名语中
修止。若于语时即知因此
语故。则有一切烦恼善恶
等法。了知语心及语中一
切烦恼。善不善法皆不可
得。则妄念心息。是名修
止。云何语中修观。应作
是念。由心觉观鼓动气
息。冲于咽喉唇舌齿

可得則妄念不起。是名修
止。云何名作時修觀。應
作是念。由心運於身。手
造作諸事。因此則有一切
善惡等法故名為作。反觀
作心不見相貌。當知作者
及作中一切法畢竟空寂。
是名修觀。六語者。若於
語時應作是念。我今為何
等事欲語。若隨諸煩惱。
為論說不善無記等事而
語。即不應語。若為善利
益事即應語。云何名語中
修止。若於語時即知因此
語故。則有一切煩惱善惡
等法。了知語心及語中一
切煩惱。善不善法皆不可
得。則妄念心息。是名修
止。云何語中修觀。應作
是念。由心覺觀鼓動氣
息。衝於咽喉唇舌齒

简体字                                                    正體字

should be completely aware that, on account of engaging in actions, there may then come to exist all of the dharmas of good, of bad, and so forth. However, if [one remains aware that] there is not one single dharma which can be gotten at, then false thoughts will not arise. It is this which constitutes the cultivation of calming.

### ii) [Insight when Engaging in Actions]

What is meant by cultivating [insight] contemplation while engaging in actions? One should bring forth this thought: "It is on account of the mind's controlling the movement of the body and hands that one engages in endeavors. It is because of this that there may then come to exist all of the dharmas of good, of bad, and so forth. Thus it is that one refers to 'engaging in actions.'"

One turns back the attention and contemplates the mind which engages in actions. One then fails to perceive any characteristic appearance. One should then realize that the agent of actions as well as all of the dharmas involved in engaging in actions are ultimately empty and still. It is this which constitutes the cultivation of [insight] contemplation.

### f) [When Speaking]

Sixth, speaking. When one is involved in speaking, one should bring forth this thought: "On account of what matter do I now wish to speak?" If one would thereby follow along with the implementation of afflictions or if it would be done for the sake of discussing matters which are unwholesome, neutral, and so forth, then one should refrain from speaking. If it is for the sake of good and beneficial matters, then one should go ahead and speak.

### i) [Calming when Speaking]

What is meant by cultivating calming when speaking? If one is engaged in speaking, one maintains the awareness that, on account of this speaking, there may then come to exist all of the dharmas of the afflictions, of good, of bad, and so forth. One becomes completely aware that the mind which engages in speaking as well as all of the dharmas of the afflictions, of good, and of bad—none of them can be found. Thus the mind which brings forth false thoughts then comes to a rest. It is this which constitutes the cultivation of calming.

### ii) [Insight when Speaking]

What is meant by cultivating contemplating in the midst of speaking?

齶故出音声语言。因此语
故则有一切善恶等法。故
名为语。反观语心不见相
貌。当知语者及语中。一
切法毕竟空寂。是名修
观。如上六义修习止观随
时相应用之。一一皆有前
五番修止观意。如上所
说。次六根门中修止观
者。一眼见色时修止者。
随见色时如水中月无有定
实。若见顺情之色不起贪
爱。若见违情之色不起瞋
恼。若见非违非顺之色。
不起无明及诸乱想。是名
修止。云何名眼见色时修
观。应作是念。随有所见
即相空寂。所以者何。于
彼根尘空明之中。

齶故出音聲語言。因此語
故則有一切善惡等法。故
名為語。反觀語心不見相
貌。當知語者及語中。一
切法畢竟空寂。是名修
觀。如上六義修習止觀隨
時相應用之。一一皆有前
五番修止觀意。如上所
說。次六根門中修止觀
者。一眼見色時修止者。
隨見色時如水中月無有定
實。若見順情之色不起貪
愛。若見違情之色不起瞋
惱。若見非違非順之色。
不起無明及諸亂想。是名
修止。云何名眼見色時修
觀。應作是念。隨有所見
即相空寂。所以者何。於
彼根塵空明之中。

简体字　　　　　　　　正體字

One should bring forth this thought: "It is based on ideation (*vitarka*) and mental discursion (*vicāra*) that one provokes the breath to move through the throat, the lips, the tongue, the teeth, and the palate. Thus one emits sound as the words of speech. It is because of this speaking that there may then come to exist the dharmas of good, of bad, and so forth. Thus it is that one refers to 'speech.'"

One turns back the attention and contemplates the mind which engages in speaking. One fails to perceive any characteristic appearance. One should then realize that the one who speaks as well as all of the dharmas involved in speaking are ultimately empty and still. It is this which constitutes the cultivation of [insight] contemplation.

g) Summation of Cultivation when Moving through Conditions

The above-discussed six sets of ideas involved in the cultivation of calming-and-insight are to be employed in a manner which adapts to whatever is appropriate at the given time. In each and every case, they also involve the five previously discussed concepts inherent in cultivating calming-and-insight. Those are to be implemented in the manner explained earlier.[11]

2) [Calming-and-Insight in Relation to Objective Spheres of the Six Senses]

Next, the cultivation of calming-and-insight at the entrances of the six sense faculties.

a) [When the Eye Views Forms]

i) [Calming when the Eye Views Forms]

First, the cultivation of calming when the eye views forms. Whenever one views forms, it is as if one were looking at the moon reflected in water. [Thus one recognizes that] there is no definite reality involved [in what one sees].

If one sees forms with which one is temperamentally agreeable, one does not give rise to desirous affection. If one sees forms to which one is temperamentally opposed, one does not give rise to hateful affliction. If one sees forms to which one is neither opposed nor agreeable, one does not manifest ignorance or any form of disordered thinking. It is this which constitutes the cultivation of calming.

ii) [Insight when the Eye Views Forms]

What is meant by the cultivation of [insight] contemplation when the eyes view form? One should think: "Whatever one observes, just

各无所见亦无分别。和合
因缘出生眼识。次生意
识。即能分别种种诸色。
因此则有一切烦恼善恶等
法。即当反观念色之心不
见相貌。当知见者及一切
法。毕竟空寂。是名修
观。二耳闻声时修止者。
随所闻声即知声如响相。
若闻顺情之声不起爱心。
违情之声不起瞋心。非违
非顺之声。不起分别心。
是名修止。云何闻声中修
观。应作是念。随所闻声
空无所有。但从根尘和合
生于耳识。次意识生强起
分别。因此即有一切烦恼
善恶等法。故名闻声。反
观闻声之心。不见相貌。
当知闻者及一切

各無所見亦無分別。和合
因緣出生眼識。次生意
識。即能分別種種諸色。
因此則有一切煩惱善惡等
法。即當反觀念色之心不
見相貌。當知見者及一切
法。畢竟空寂。是名修
觀。二耳聞聲時修止者。
隨所聞聲即知聲如響相。
若聞順情之聲不起愛心。
違情之聲不起瞋心。非違
非順之聲。不起分別心。
是名修止。云何聞聲中修
觀。應作是念。隨所聞聲
空無所有。但從根塵和合
生於耳識。次意識生強起
分別。因此即有一切煩惱
善惡等法。故名聞聲。反
觀聞聲之心。不見相貌。
當知聞者及一切

简体字 　　　　　　　　　 正體字

those very characteristic features are themselves empty [of inherent existence] and abiding in stillness. How is this the case? Within the sphere of that sense faculty, sense object, space, and light, there is nothing seen on the part of any one of them, nor is there any discrimination which takes place therein.

"Rather it is a combination of causes and conditions which generates eye consciousness. Next, there occurs the arising of the mind consciousness. That is then immediately able to make distinctions among all of the various types of forms. It is on account of this that there may then come to exist all of the dharmas of the afflictions, of good, of bad, and so forth."

One should immediately turn the attention back and contemplate that mind which bears forms in mind. One does not then perceive that it possesses any characteristic appearance. One should then realize that the one who sees as well as all of the other associated dharmas are ultimately empty [of inherent existence] and abiding in stillness. It is this which constitutes the cultivation of [insight] contemplation.

b) [WHEN THE EAR HEARS SOUNDS]
i) [CALMING WHEN THE EAR HEARS SOUNDS]

Second, the cultivation of calming when the ear hears sounds. Whichever sounds are heard by the ear, one immediately realizes that the sounds are characterized by being like echoes.

If one hears sounds with which one is temperamentally agreeable, one does not give rise to an affectionate mind. As for sounds to which one is temperamentally opposed, one does not give rise to a hateful mind. And as for sounds to which one is neither opposed nor agreeable, one does not give rise to a discriminating mind. It is this which constitutes the cultivation of calming.

ii) [INSIGHT WHEN THE EAR HEARS SOUNDS]

What is meant by the cultivation of [insight] contemplation in the hearing of sounds? One should bring forth this thought: "No matter what sound is heard, it is empty and utterly devoid of any [inherent] existence. It is only from the coming together of the sense faculty and the sense object that there is the generation of ear consciousness. Next, the mind consciousness arises and, in a forced manner, gives rise to discriminations. It is because of this that there may then come to exist all of the dharmas of the afflictions, of good, of bad, and so forth."

法。毕竟空寂。是名为
观。三鼻嗅香时修止者。
随所闻香即知如焰不实。
若闻顺情之香不起着心。
违情之臭不起瞋心。非违
非顺之香不生乱念。是名
修止。云何名闻香中修
观。应作是念。我今闻香
虚诳无实。所以者何。根
尘合故而生鼻识。次生意
识强取香相。因此则有一
切烦恼善恶等法。故名闻
香。反观闻香之心。不见
相貌。当知闻香及一切法
毕竟空寂。是名修观。四
舌受味时修止者。随所受
味即知如于梦幻中得味。
若得顺情美味不起贪着。
违情恶味不起瞋心。

簡体字

法。畢竟空寂。是名為
觀。三鼻嗅香時修止者。
隨所聞香即知如焰不實。
若聞順情之香不起著心。
違情之臭不起瞋心。非違
非順之香不生亂念。是名
修止。云何名聞香中修
觀。應作是念。我今聞香
虛誑無實。所以者何。根
塵合故而生鼻識。次生意
識強取香相。因此則有一
切煩惱善惡等法。故名聞
香。反觀聞香之心。不見
相貌。當知聞香及一切法
畢竟空寂。是名修觀。四
舌受味時修止者。隨所受
味即知如於夢幻中得味。
若得順情美味不起貪著。
違情惡味不起瞋心。

正體字

One turns back the attention and contemplates the mind which hears sounds. One does not perceive any characteristic appearance. One should then realize that the one who hears as well as all of the other associated dharmas are ultimately empty and still. It is this which constitutes [insight] contemplation.

c) [WHEN THE NOSE SMELLS FRAGRANCES]
i) [CALMING WHEN THE NOSE SMELLS FRAGRANCES]

Third, the cultivation of calming when the nose smells fragrances. No matter what fragrances are smelled, one immediately realizes that they are like flames and are unreal. If one smells fragrances with which one is temperamentally agreeable, one does not give rise to a mind characterized by attachment. As for smells to which one is temperamentally opposed, one does not give rise to a hateful mind. And as for smells towards which one is neither opposed nor agreeable, one does not bring forth disordered thinking. It is this which constitutes the cultivation of calming.

ii) [INSIGHT WHEN THE NOSE SMELLS FRAGRANCES]

What is meant by the cultivation of [insight] contemplation in the smelling of fragrances? One should bring forth this thought: "The fragrances which I am now smelling are false, deceptive, and unreal. How is this the case? It is because of the coming together of the sense faculty and the sense object that there is then produced the olfactory consciousness. Next, there is the production of the mind consciousness. In a forced manner, it then seizes upon the characteristics of fragrances. It is because of this that there may then come to exist all of the dharmas of the afflictions, of good, of bad, and so forth. Thus it is that we speak of 'smelling fragrances.'"

One turns back the attention and contemplates the mind which smells fragrances. One does not perceive that it possesses any characteristic appearance. One should then realize that the one who smells fragrances as well as all of the other associated dharmas are ultimately empty [of inherent existence] and abiding in stillness. It is this which constitutes the cultivation of [insight] contemplation.

d) [WHEN THE TONGUE TASTES FLAVORS]
i) [CALMING WHEN THE TONGUE TASTES FLAVORS]

Fourth, the cultivation of calming when the tongue tastes flavors. No matter what flavors are tasted, one immediately realizes that they are like flavors tasted in a dream or as part of a conjuration.

非违非顺之味。不起分别意想。是名修止。云何名舌受味时修观。应作是念。今所受味实不可得。所以者何。内外六味性无分别。因内舌根和合则舌识生。次生意识强取味相。因此则有一切烦恼善恶等法。反观缘味之识不见相貌。当知受味者及一切法。毕竟空寂。是名修观五身受触时修止者。随所觉触即知如影幻化不实。若受顺情乐触不起贪着。若受违情苦触不起瞋恼。受非违非顺之触。不起忆想分别。是名修止。云何身受触时修观。应作是念。

简体字

非違非順之味。不起分別意想。是名修止。云何名舌受味時修觀。應作是念。今所受味實不可得。所以者何。內外六味性無分別。因內舌根和合則舌識生。次生意識強取味相。因此則有一切煩惱善惡等法。反觀緣味之識不見相貌。當知受味者及一切法。畢竟空寂。是名修觀五身受觸時修止者。隨所覺觸即知如影幻化不實。若受順情樂觸不起貪著。若受違情苦觸不起瞋惱。受非違非順之觸。不起憶想分別。是名修止。云何身受觸時修觀。應作是念。

正體字

If one obtains a marvelous flavor towards which one is temperamentally agreeable, one does not give rise to desirous attachment. As for bad tastes towards which one is temperamentally opposed, one does not give rise to a hateful mind. And as for tastes towards which one is neither opposed nor agreeable, one does not give rise to discriminating thoughts on the part of the intellectual mind. It is this which constitutes the cultivation of calming.

ii) [INSIGHT WHEN THE TONGUE TASTES FLAVORS]

What is meant by cultivating [insight] contemplation when the tongue experiences tastes? One should bring forth this thought: "In reality, the tastes which are now being experienced cannot be apprehended as existents. How is this so? The subjective and objective factors involved in the six flavors are by their very nature free of any discriminating function. It is because one's tongue organ comes into conjunction with them that gustatory consciousness arises. Next, one gives rise to mind consciousness. That then seizes in a forced manner upon the characteristic aspects of flavors. It is because of this that there may then come to exist all of the dharmas of the afflictions, of good, of bad, and so forth."

One turns back the attention and contemplates the consciousness which takes tastes as its objective conditions. One does not perceive any characteristic appearance. One should then realize that the one who experiences tastes as well as all of the other associated dharmas are ultimately empty [of inherent existence] and abiding in stillness. It is this which constitutes the cultivation of [insight] contemplation.

e) [WHEN THE BODY ENGAGES TANGIBLES]

i) [CALMING WHEN THE BODY ENGAGES TANGIBLES]

Fifth, the cultivation of calming when the body engages tangibles. No matter which tactile sensations become the object of awareness, one immediately realizes that they are like a reflection, like an illusion, or like a conjuration, and thus are unreal.

If one experiences a pleasurable tactile sensation to which one is temperamentally agreeable, one does not give rise to desirous attachment. If one experiences painful tactile sensations to which one is temperamentally opposed, one does not give rise to hateful affliction. If one experiences tactile sensations to which one is neither opposed nor agreeable, one does not give rise to thoughts

轻重冷暖澀滑等法。名之
为触。头等六分名之为
身。触性虚假身亦不实。
和合因缘即生身识。次生
意识忆想分别苦乐等相。
故名受触。反观缘触之心
不见相貌。当知受触者及
一切法。毕竟空寂。是名
修观。六意知法中修止观
相。如初坐中已明讫。自
上依六根。修止观相。随
所意用而用之。一一具上
五番之意。是中已广分
别。今不重辨。行者若能
于行住坐卧。见闻觉知等
一切处中。修止观者。当
知是人真修摩诃衍道。如
大品经云。佛告须菩提。
若菩萨行时知行。坐时知
坐。乃至服僧伽梨。视眴
一心出入禅定。当知是人
名菩萨摩诃衍。

輕重冷暖澀滑等法。名之
為觸。頭等六分名之為
身。觸性虛假身亦不實。
和合因緣即生身識。次生
意識憶想分別苦樂等相。
故名受觸。反觀緣觸之心
不見相貌。當知受觸者及
一切法。畢竟空寂。是名
修觀。六意知法中修止觀
相。如初坐中已明訖。自
上依六根。修止觀相。隨
所意用而用之。一一具上
五番之意。是中已廣分
別。今不重辨。行者若能
於行住坐臥。見聞覺知等
一切處中。修止觀者。當
知是人真修摩訶衍道。如
大品經云。佛告須菩提。
若菩薩行時知行。坐時知
坐。乃至服僧伽梨。視眴
一心出入禪定。當知是人
名菩薩摩訶衍。

简体字                    正體字

which retain them in mind nor does one engage in making distinctions among them. This constitutes the cultivation of calming.

### ii) [INSIGHT WHEN THE BODY ENGAGES TANGIBLES]

What is meant by the cultivation of [insight] contemplation when the body engages tangibles? One should bring forth this thought: "Lightness and heaviness, coolness and heat, roughness and slickness and other such dharmas are all tactile sensations. The six sections of the body consisting of the head and so forth constitute what is referred to as the body. The nature of tactile sensations is that they are empty and false. The body, too, is unreal. It is through the coming together of causes and conditions that there is the arising of physical consciousness. There next arises the mind consciousness which engages in recollective thought and the making of distinctions with regard to the characteristics of pleasure, pain, and so forth. Thus it is that we speak of 'experiencing tactile sensations.'"

One turns back the attention and contemplates the mind which takes tactile sensations as objective conditions. One does not perceive it to possess any characteristic appearance. One should then realize that the one who experiences tactile sensations as well as all of the other associated dharmas are ultimately empty [of inherent existence] and abiding in stillness. It is this which constitutes the cultivation of [insight] contemplation.

### f) [WHEN THE MIND EXPERIENCES AWARENESS OF DHARMAS]

Sixth, the features of the cultivation of calming-and-insight in the midst of the mind's awareness of dharmas are as already explained at the beginning [of this chapter], in the section devoted to sitting meditation. From among the above features relating to the cultivation of calming-and-insight in dependence upon the six sense faculties, one implements whichever ones correspond to that faculty which one intends to utilize. The five concepts discussed earlier are inherent in each and every one of these situations.[12] Because they have already been extensively detailed herein, we won't repeat the analysis now.

### c. [THE BENEFITS AND SCRIPTURAL CITATIONS]

If the practitioner is able to cultivate calming-and-insight at every point as he walks, stands, sits, lies down, sees, hears, experiences awareness, and so forth, then one ought to know that this person truly cultivates the Mahāyāna path. As stated in the *Large Sutra*,

| | |
|---|---|
| 复次若人能如是。一切处中修行大乘。是人则于世间最胜最上。无与等者。释论偈中说 | 復次若人能如是。一切處中修行大乘。是人則於世間最勝最上。無與等者。釋論偈中說 |

| | | | |
|---|---|---|---|
| 闲坐林树间 | 寂然灭诸恶 | 閑坐林樹間 | 寂然滅諸惡 |
| 憺怕得一心 | 斯乐非天乐 | 憺怕得一心 | 斯樂非天樂 |
| 人求世间利 | 名衣好床褥 | 人求世間利 | 名衣好床褥 |
| 斯乐非安隐 | 求利无厌足 | 斯樂非安隱 | 求利無厭足 |
| 衲衣在空闲 | 动止心常一 | 衲衣在空閑 | 動止心常一 |
| 自以智慧明 | 观诸法实相 | 自以智慧明 | 觀諸法實相 |
| 种种诸法中 | 皆以等观入 | 種種諸法中 | 皆以等觀入 |
| 解慧心寂然 | 三界无伦匹 | 解慧心寂然 | 三界無倫匹 |

简体字　　　　　　　　　正體字

"The Buddha told Subhūti, 'If when the bodhisattva walks, he is aware of walking, if when he sits, he is aware of sitting...'" and so forth until we come to "...when he dons the *saṅghāṭī* robe, ...gazes, or blinks, ...he is single-minded, ...both exiting from and entering into dhyāna absorption...".[13] One should know that a person such as this qualifies as a bodhisattva, a Mahāyānist.

Furthermore, if a person is able to cultivate the Great Vehicle in this manner in every situation, this person is the most superior in all the world. He is the most supreme and has no peer. A verse from the [*Mahāprajñāpāramitā*] *Upadeśa* states:

> Easefully sitting within the forest,
> Quiescently extinguishing every ill,
> Serenely gaining unity of mind—
> This bliss is not the bliss of the heavens.

> People seek after worldly profit,
> Fame, robes, and fine beds and cushions.
> Bliss of this sort is not secure.
> In seeking profit, there is no satisfaction.

> The patch-robed one abides in deserted places.
> Moving and stopping, his mind is always one.
> Spontaneously employing the clarity of wisdom,
> He contemplates the true character of dharmas.

> In all of the different classes of dharmas,
> All are entered through [insight] contemplation of their equality.
> The mind of understanding wisdom abides in quiescence.
> Throughout the three realms, there are none ranked as peer.[14]

| 善根发第七 | 善根發第七 |
|---|---|
| [0469b03] 行者若能如是。从假入空观中。善修止观者。则于坐中身心明净。尔时当有种种善根开发。应须识知。今略明善根发相。有二种不同。一外善根发相。所谓布施持戒孝顺父母尊长。供养三宝及诸听学等。善根开发。此是外事。若非正修。与魔境相滥。今不分别。二内善根发相。所谓诸禅定法门善根开发。有三种意。第一明善根发相有五种不同。一息道善根发相。 | [0469b03] 行者若能如是。從假入空觀中。善修止觀者。則於坐中身心明淨。爾時當有種種善根開發。應須識知。今略明善根發相。有二種不同。一外善根發相。所謂布施持戒孝順父母尊長。供養三寶及諸聽學等。善根開發。此是外事。若非正修。與魔境相滥。今不分別。二內善根發相。所謂諸禪定法門善根開發。有三種意。第一明善根發相有五種不同。一息道善根發相。 |
| 简体字 | 正體字 |

# CHAPTER SEVEN
## Manifestations of Roots of Goodness

7. SECTION SEVEN: MANIFESTATIONS OF ROOTS OF GOODNESS

If the practitioner is able in this manner to skillfully cultivate calming-and-insight, going from the [insight] contemplation of the conventional into the [insight] contemplation of emptiness, as he sits in meditation, his body and mind will manifest as bright and pure.[1] At such time, there may occur the development and manifestation of many different sorts of roots of goodness (kuśala-mūla). One must recognize and be aware of them.

Now, we shall briefly explain the signs associated with the manifestation of roots of goodness. This involves two different categories, as follows.

### a. [OUTWARD ROOTS OF GOODNESS]

First, the signs associated with the manifestation of "outward" roots of goodness: This refers to the development and manifestation of roots of goodness associated with giving, upholding moral precepts, filial dutifulness to parents, veneration of seniors, making offerings to the Triple Jewel, listening to and studying the teachings, and so forth. These are outward matters.[2]

If one is not engaged in correct cultivation, it may happen that there is a mutual spilling over and admixture with demonic states of mind. We will not now analyze these matters in detail.[3]

### b. [INWARD ROOTS OF GOODNESS]

Second, the signs of the manifestation of "inward" roots of goodness. This refers to the development and manifestation of roots of goodness related to the Dharma gateways associated with the dhyāna absorptions. There are three concepts to be considered here.

#### 1) [SIGNS OF MANIFESTATION OF ROOTS OF GOODNESS]

The first, the explanation of the signs of the manifestation of roots of goodness. This involves five different categories, as follows.

##### a) [SIGNS RELATED TO PATHWAYS OF THE BREATH]

First, the signs related to the manifestation of roots of goodness linked to the pathways of the breath. On account of the practitioner's

行者善修止观故。身心调适妄念止息。因是自觉其心渐渐入定。发于欲界及未到地等定。身心泯然空寂定心安隐。于此定中都不见有身心相貌。于后或经一坐二坐。乃至一日二日。一月二月。将息不得不退不失。即于定中忽觉身心运动八触而发者。所谓觉身痛痒冷煖轻重濇滑等。当触发时身心安定虚微悦豫。快乐清净不可为喻。是为知息道根本禅定善根发相。行者或于欲界未到地中。忽然觉息出入长短。遍身毛孔皆悉虚疎。即以心眼见身内三十六物。犹如开仓见诸麻豆等。心大惊喜。寂静安快。是为随息特胜善根发相。二不净观善根发相。行者若于

简体字

行者善修止觀故。身心調適妄念止息。因是自覺其心漸漸入定。發於欲界及未到地等定。身心泯然空寂定心安隱。於此定中都不見有身心相貌。於後或經一坐二坐。乃至一日二日。一月二月。將息不得不退不失。即於定中忽覺身心運動八觸而發者。所謂覺身痛痒冷煖輕重濇滑等。當觸發時身心安定虛微悅豫。快樂清淨不可為喻。是為知息道根本禪定善根發相。行者或於欲界未到地中。忽然覺息出入長短。遍身毛孔皆悉虛疎。即以心眼見身內三十六物。猶如開倉見諸麻豆等。心大驚喜。寂靜安快。是為隨息特勝善根發相。二不淨觀善根發相。行者若於

正體字

skillful cultivation of calming-and-insight, the body and mind become regulated correctly and false thinking comes to a halt. Because of this, one becomes aware that one's mind gradually enters into meditative absorption. These phenomena manifest in desire realm absorptions and the "preliminary-ground" (*anāgamya*).[4]

The body and mind seem as if they have disappeared and are experienced as empty and quiescent. The mind associated with meditative absorption becomes peaceful and stable. In the midst of this meditative absorption, one does not perceive any appearance whatsoever of a body or a mind. Then, afterwards, one may continue on through one or two sitting sessions, and so forth until we come to one day, two days, one month, or two months. In attempting to take up with [cultivation focused on] the breath, one may find it to be imperceptible. It may be that this circumstance does not recede and is not lost.

Then, in the midst of meditative absorption, one may suddenly become aware of the body and mind moving and provoking the manifestation of eight tactile sensations, namely the awareness of physical pain, itching, coldness, heat, lightness, heaviness, roughness, smoothness, and so forth.

At that time when there is the manifestation of these dharmas of tactile sensation, the body and mind are peaceful and stabilized. There is an empty and subtle blissfulness. One's happiness and pleasure are pure and indescribable even by simile. These are signs of the manifestation of roots of goodness characterized by the basic dhyāna absorption's awareness of the pathways of breath.

It may be that, in the preliminary ground of the desire realm, the practitioner suddenly becomes aware of the exiting and entry of the breath, of its relative duration, and of its pervading the entire body, coursing emptily through all of one's hair pores. One then immediately sees with the mind's eye the thirty-six categories of physical components contained within the body just as when, upon opening up a pantry, one sees all of the sesame seeds, beans, and so forth. The mind is both profoundly startled and delighted. One becomes quiescent, peaceful, and happy. These are signs of the manifestation of roots of goodness corresponding to the special ascendant practices associated with the breath.[5]

b) [SIGNS RELATED TO CONTEMPLATION OF IMPURITY]

Second, the signs of the manifestation of roots of goodness related to the contemplation of impurity. When the practitioner is immersed in

欲界未到地定。于此定中
身心虚寂。忽然见他男女
身死。死已膖胀烂坏虫脓
流出。见白骨狼藉。其心
悲喜厌患所爱。此为九想
善根发相。或于静定之
中。忽然见内身不净。外
身膖胀狼藉。自身白骨从
头至足。节节相拄。见是
事已。定心安隐惊悟无
常。厌患五欲不着我人。
此是背舍善根发相。或于
定心中。见于内身及外
身。一切飞禽走兽。衣服
饮食屋舍山林。皆悉不
净。此为大不净善根发
相。三慈心善根发相。行
者因修止观故。若得欲界
未到地定于此定中忽然发
心慈念众生。或缘亲人得
乐之相。即发深定。

欲界未到地定。於此定中
身心虛寂。忽然見他男女
身死。死已膖脹爛壞蟲膿
流出。見白骨狼藉。其心
悲喜厭患所愛。此為九想
善根發相。或於靜定之
中。忽然見內身不淨。外
身膖脹狼藉。自身白骨從
頭至足。節節相拄。見是
事已。定心安隱驚悟無
常。厭患五欲不著我人。
此是背捨善根發相。或於
定心中。見於內身及外
身。一切飛禽走獸。衣服
飲食屋舍山林。皆悉不
淨。此為大不淨善根發
相。三慈心善根發相。行
者因修止觀故。若得欲界
未到地定於此定中忽然發
心慈念眾生。或緣親人得
樂之相。即發深定。

简体字　　　　　　正體字

the meditative absorption of the desire realm's preliminary ground, his body and mind become empty and still in the midst of this meditative absorption, [whereupon he may experience the following signs]: He may suddenly observe an appearance of the physical death of some other man or woman and then, following upon that death, the corpse's bloating and rotting, the presence of worms, and the flowing forth of pus. He may then observe the whitened bones scattered about. His mind may become affected by sorrow and delight and he may then experience revulsion and abhorrence for that which he had previously loved. These are signs indicating the manifestation of roots of goodness related to the nine reflections.[6]

Then again, it may happen that, in the midst of quiescent meditative absorption, one may suddenly observe the impure things inside of the body, someone else's body as bloated and scattered, or his own body as a white skeleton from the head to foot, with every one of the bones held in position by the others. After having seen this phenomenon, the mind of absorption may become peaceful and stable. One may experience a startling awakening to a realization of impermanence. One may then develop revulsion and abhorrence for the five objects of desire, and may then desist from attachment to either oneself or other persons. These are signs of the manifestation of roots of goodness related to the [eight] liberations.[7]

Then again, when the mind is immersed in meditative absorption, one may observe everything as utterly impure, maintaining this perception whether it be with regard to one's own body, the bodies of others, flying birds, crawling beasts, clothing, drink, food, dwellings, mountains, or forests. These are signs indicating the manifestation of roots of goodness related to [past-life contemplation of] the great [all-encompassing] impurity.

c) [Signs Related to the Mind of Loving-kindness]

Third, the signs of the manifestation of roots of goodness related to the mind of loving-kindness (*maitrī*). If, on account of cultivating calming-and-insight, the practitioner succeeds in entering the meditative absorption of the desire realm's preliminary ground (*anāgamya*), while he is immersed in this meditative absorption, he may suddenly bring forth a mind characterized by a lovingly-kind mindfulness of other beings wherein there appear to him signs indicating that persons with whom he has close affinities gain happiness. He may then immediately develop deep meditative

内心悦乐清净不可为喻。
中人怨人乃至十方五道众
生。亦复如是。从禅定起
其心悦乐。随所见人颜色
常和。是为慈心善根发
相。悲喜舍心发相。类此
可知也。四因缘观善根发
相。行者因修止观故。若
得欲界未到地。身心静
定。忽然觉悟心生。推寻
三世无明行等诸因缘中不
见人我。即离断常。破诸
执见。得定安隐解慧开
发。心生法喜不念世间之
事。乃至五阴十二处十八
界中。分别亦如是。是为
因缘观善根发相。五念佛
善根发相。行者因修

簡体字

内心悅樂清淨不可為喻。
中人怨人乃至十方五道眾
生。亦復如是。從禪定起
其心悅樂。隨所見人顏色
常和。是為慈心善根發
相。悲喜捨心發相。類此
可知也。四因緣觀善根發
相。行者因修止觀故。若
得欲界未到地。身心靜
定。忽然覺悟心生。推尋
三世無明行等諸因緣中不
見人我。即離斷常。破諸
執見。得定安隱解慧開
發。心生法喜不念世間之
事。乃至五陰十二處十八
界中。分別亦如是。是為
因緣觀善根發相。五念佛
善根發相。行者因修

正體字

absorption wherein his own mind manifests a pure and blissful happiness indescribable even by simile.

Identical experiences may occur [for the practitioner] in relation to people towards whom he possesses only middling affinities, in relation to people who have been his adversaries and, ultimately, even in relation to all of the beings within the five rebirth destinies throughout the ten directions. When he arises from meditative absorption, his mind abides in blissful happiness, so much so that, no matter whom he sees, his countenance remains constantly harmonious. These are signs of the manifestation of roots of goodness related to the mind of loving-kindness. The signs of the manifestation of the mind of compassion (*karuṇa*), the mind of sympathetic joy (*muditā*), and the mind of equanimity (*upekṣā*) may all be understood through comparison to this.[8]

d) [Signs Related to Contemplation of Causes and Conditions]

Fourth, the signs of the manifestation of roots of goodness related to the contemplation of causes and conditions. It may be that, on account of cultivating calming-and-insight, the practitioner gains the desire realm's preliminary-ground meditative absorption in which the body and mind abide in stillness. He may then suddenly experience the arising of an awakened mind wherein, in pursuing deliberation upon the causes and conditions of ignorance, karmic formative factors (*saṃskāras*), and so forth as they play out in the three periods of time, he does not perceive the [inherent] existence of either others or a self.[9]

[The practitioner may] then immediately transcend [views positing] annihilationism and eternalism, demolish all attachments and views, and gain the peace and security of meditative absorption. Understanding and wisdom may manifest, Dharma joy may come forth in his mind, and his thought may remain free of concerns associated with worldly matters.

As for the distinctions involved in one's experiences in relation to the five aggregates, the twelve sense bases, and the eighteen sense realms, they may be of a character similar to the above. These are signs of the manifestation of roots of goodness related to the contemplation of causes and conditions.

e) [Signs Related to Mindfulness of the Buddha]

Fifth, the signs of the manifestation of roots of goodness related to mindfulness of the Buddha. It may be that, on account of cultivating

止观故。若得欲界未到地定。身心空寂。忽然忆念诸佛功德相好。不可思议所有十力。无畏。不共。三昧。解脱等法。不可思议神通变化。无碍说法广利众生。不可思议。如是等无量功德。不可思议。作是念时即发爱敬心生。三昧开发身心快乐。清净安隐无诸恶相。从禅定起身体轻利。自觉功德巍巍人所爱敬。是为念佛三昧善根发相。复次行者因修止观故。若得身心澄净。或发无常苦空无我不净。世间可厌食不净相。死离尽想。念佛法僧戒舍天。念处正勤如意根力觉道。空无相无作。六度诸波罗蜜神通变化等。一切法门发相。是中应广分别。故经云。制心

止觀故。若得欲界未到地定。身心空寂。忽然憶念諸佛功德相好。不可思議所有十力。無畏。不共。三昧。解脫等法。不可思議神通變化。無礙說法廣利眾生。不可思議。如是等無量功德。不可思議。作是念時即發愛敬心生。三昧開發身心快樂。清淨安隱無諸惡相。從禪定起身體輕利。自覺功德巍巍人所愛敬。是為念佛三昧善根發相。復次行者因修止觀故。若得身心澄淨。或發無常苦空無我不淨。世間可厭食不淨相。死離盡想。念佛法僧戒捨天。念處正勤如意根力覺道。空無相無作。六度諸波羅蜜神通變化等。一切法門發相。是中應廣分別。故經云。制心

简体字　　　　　　　正體字

calming-and-insight, the practitioner gains the desire realm's preliminary-ground meditative absorption wherein his body and mind become empty and still. It may be that he then immediately calls to mind the inconceivable and ineffable meritorious qualities and major and minor characteristics of the Buddha, including all of the ten powers, the fearlessnesses, the dharmas exclusive to the Buddha, the samādhis, the liberations, and other such dharmas, including also the inconceivable and indescribable superknowledges and transformations, and including also the unimpeded eloquences and vast benefits to beings which are themselves so inconceivable and indescribable.

When [the practitioner] engages in such thought, he then manifests a mind imbued with admiring reverence. Samādhi develops in him. Thus his body and mind become blissful, pure, peaceful, and secure, and he becomes free of any unwholesome characteristics.

When he arises from dhyāna absorption, his body abides in a state of lightness and easefulness (*praśrabhi*).[10] He realizes for himself that [the Buddha's] meritorious qualities are lofty and impressive and that they are fit to be the object of a person's admiring reverence. These are signs of the manifestation of roots of goodness related to the mindfulness-of-the-Buddha samādhi.

f)  [SIGNS RELATED TO OTHER ROOTS OF GOODNESS]

Furthermore, in the event that the practitioner gains clarity and purity of body and mind on account of cultivating calming-and-insight, he may then experience the manifestation of signs associated with the reflections on impermanence, suffering, emptiness, non-self, impurity, renunciability of the world, impurity of food, death, abandonment, or cessation, or he may experience signs associated with the recollections of the Buddha, of the Dharma, of the Sangha, of the precepts, of relinquishing, or of the heavens.[11]

[The practitioner] may experience the manifestation of signs associated with any of the Dharma entryways, including the stations of mindfulness, the right efforts, the foundations of psychic power, the roots, the powers, the limbs of enlightenment, or the [eight-fold] path,[12] or may experience signs associated with emptiness, signlessness, wishlessness,[13] the six perfections, any of the [other] pāramitās,[14] the superknowledges and transformations, and so forth. Ideally, these should all be analyzed extensively herein. Thus it is that a sutra states: "If one controls the mind so that it

一处无事不办。二分别真
伪者。有二。一者辨邪伪
禅发相。行者若发如上诸
禅时。随因所发之法或身
搔动。或时身重如物镇
压。或时身轻欲飞。或时
如缚。或时逶迤垂熟。或
时煎寒。或时壮热。或见
种种诸异境界。或时其心
暗蔽。或时起诸恶觉。或
时念外散乱诸杂善事。或
时欢喜躁动。或时忧愁悲
思。或时恶触身毛惊竖。
或时大乐昏醉。如是种种
邪法。与禅俱发。名为邪
伪。此之邪定若人爱着。
即与九十五种鬼神法相
应。多好失心颠狂。或时
诸鬼神等知人念着其法。
即加势力令发诸邪定。

一處無事不辦。二分別真
偽者。有二。一者辨邪偽
禪發相。行者若發如上諸
禪時。隨因所發之法或身
搔動。或時身重如物鎮
壓。或時身輕欲飛。或時
如縛。或時逶迤垂熟。或
時煎寒。或時壯熱。或見
種種諸異境界。或時其心
闇蔽。或時起諸惡覺。或
時念外散亂諸雜善事。或
時歡喜躁動。或時憂愁悲
思。或時惡觸身毛驚竪。
或時大樂昏醉。如是種種
邪法。與禪俱發。名為邪
偽。此之邪定若人愛著。
即與九十五種鬼神法相
應。多好失心顛狂。或時
諸鬼神等知人念著其法。
即加勢力令發諸邪定。

简体字                        正體字

abides in a single place, there is no endeavor which may not be accomplished."[15]

2) [DISTINGUISHING BETWEEN TRUE AND FALSE]

Second, the section on "distinguishing between the true and the false," consists itself of two parts.

a) [SIGNS OF FALSE DHYĀNA ABSORPTIONS]

The first part is "describing the signs of the manifestation of false dhyāna absorptions."

When the practitioner experiences the manifestation of dhyāna absorptions such as discussed above, it may be that, on account of the dharmas which have become manifest, [he experiences the following]: It may be that the body manifests agitated movement. At times the body may feel heavy, as if something was pressing down and smashing it. At times the body may feel light, as if it was about to fly. At times it might feel as if it were tied up. At times it may feel as if one were twisting around, being suspended while roasted. Or at times it may feel as if one were being subjected to boiling or cold. At times one may experience intensely strong heat.

Or perhaps one might see all sorts of strange mental states. At times one's mind may become dark and covered over. Sometimes one may generate all sorts of evil ideations. Sometimes one may bring to mind external scatteredness and confusion associated with miscellaneous wholesome endeavors. Sometimes one may experience delight or agitated movement. Sometimes one may become worried or preoccupied with sad thoughts. Sometimes one may experience unwholesome tactile sensations causing the hairs on the body to stand on end. Sometimes one may become so intensely happy that one acts confused or inebriated. All sorts of abnormal dharmas such as these, when manifesting together with dhyāna absorption, amount to instances of aberrant falseness.

If one becomes affectionately attached to these deviant meditative absorptions, then one accords with the dharmas of the ninety-five kinds of ghosts and spirits. One then becomes increasingly inclined towards mental derangement associated with the loss of one's mind [of correct resolve]. Sometimes the ghosts, spirits, and other such beings become aware that a person has become mentally attached to their dharmas. Consequently they then immediately increase the intensity of the power [associated with those dharmas] such that one then manifests all sorts of aberrant meditative absorptions

邪智辩才神通惑动世人。凡愚见者谓得道果皆悉信伏。而其内心颠倒专行鬼法惑乱世间。是人命终永不值佛。还堕鬼神道中。若坐时多行恶法。即堕地狱。行者修止观时。若证如是等禅有此诸邪伪相。当即却之。云何却之。若知虚诳正心不受不着即当谢灭。应用正观破之即当灭矣。二者辨真正禅发相。行者若于坐中发诸禅时。无有如上所说诸邪法等。随一一禅发时。即觉与定相应。空明清净内心喜悦憺然快乐。无有覆盖。善心开发信敬增长。智鉴分明身心柔软微妙虚寂。厌患

邪智辯才神通惑動世人。凡愚見者謂得道果皆悉信伏。而其內心顛倒專行鬼法惑亂世間。是人命終永不值佛。還墮鬼神道中。若坐時多行惡法。即墮地獄。行者修止觀時。若證如是等禪有此諸邪偽相。當即却之。云何却之。若知虛誑正心不受不著即當謝滅。應用正觀破之即當滅矣。二者辨真正禪發相。行者若於坐中發諸禪時。無有如上所說諸邪法等。隨一一禪發時。即覺與定相應。空明清淨內心喜悅憺然快樂。無有覆蓋。善心開發信敬增長。智鑒分明身心柔軟微妙虛寂。厭患

简体字　　　　　　　　正體字

and aberrant forms of intelligence, eloquence, and spiritual powers through which one might then fall into influencing people of the world through deception.

When the common foolish person observes this, he is of the opinion that one has gained the fruit of coursing along the Path. They all believe in and submit to such a person even though his mind is possessed by inverted views, even though he exclusively practices the dharmas of ghosts, and even though he deceives and confuses the inhabitants of the world.

When such a person's life comes to an end, he will remain forever unable to encounter the Buddha and will fall back down into the path of the ghosts and spirits. If he has mostly engaged in the practice of evil dharmas when sitting in meditation, he will immediately fall into the hells.

If, when the practitioner cultivates calming-and-insight, he achieves dhyāna absorptions like these which are possessed of these signs of falseness, he should then immediately get rid of them. How does one get rid of them? If one becomes aware of the presence of falseness and deception, he should establish himself in correctness of mind and desist from accepting or becoming attached to them. They should then diminish and disappear. If one implements correct contemplation to demolish them, they should then immediately disappear.

b) [Signs of True, Correct Dhyāna Absorption]

Second, "articulating the signs of the manifestation of true and correct dhyāna absorption." [This refers to] when the practitioner is engaged in sitting meditation and there manifest dhyāna absorptions wherein there are none of the above-described abnormal dharmas. When each and every dhyāna absorption manifests, one immediately becomes aware of its relationship to meditative absorption.

One experiences emptiness, brightness, and purity. Inwardly, one's mind is delighted. One feels tranquil and blissful. There are no situations wherein one is covered over by the hindrances. The mind of goodness comes forth and manifests.

One's faith and reverence increase and grow. One's mirror of wisdom becomes clear and bright. The body and mind become supple and pliant. One experiences a subtle and marvelous emptiness and quiescence. One develops a revulsion for and abhorrence

世间无为无欲出入自在。
是为正禅发相。譬如与恶
人共事恒相触恼。若与善
人共事久见其美。分别邪
正二种禅发之相。亦复如
是。三明用止观长养诸善
根者。若于坐中诸善根发
时。应用止观二法修令增
进。　若宜用止则以止修
之。　若宜用观则以观修
之。具如前说略示大意[1]
矣

世間無為無欲出入自在。
是為正禪發相。譬如與惡
人共事恒相觸惱。若與善
人共事久見其美。分別邪
正二種禪發之相。亦復如
是。三明用止觀長養諸善
根者。若於坐中諸善根發
時。應用止觀二法修令增
進。　若宜用止則以止修
之。　若宜用觀則以觀修
之。具如前說略示大意[1]
矣

简体字　　　　　　　　正體字

of the world. There is nothing [which one feels needs] to be done and one remains free of desires. One remains sovereignly independent in one's ability to emerge from and enter into [meditative absorption].

These are the signs of the manifestation of correct dhyāna absorptions. This is just as when working with evil people, one constantly encounters mutual aggravation, whereas when working together with good people, one eventually observes their fine points. It is much the same in distinguishing the deviant and the correct, the two types of signs manifesting in cultivating dhyāna absorption.

    c)  [INCREASING GROWTH OF ROOTS OF GOODNESS]

Third, "clarifying the use of calming-and-insight to increase the growth of roots of goodness." When one is sitting [in meditation] and roots of goodness manifest, one should employ the two dharmas of calming and insight to cultivate them and cause them to increase and advance. If it is appropriate to employ calming, then one uses calming to cultivate them. If it is appropriate to employ insight, then one uses [insight] contemplation to cultivate them. One does this in a manner which accords with the previous discussions. This has been a summary explanation of the major ideas [related to this topic].

## 觉知魔事第八

[0470b02] 　　梵音魔罗。秦言杀者。夺行人功德之财。杀行人智慧之命。是故名之为恶魔。事者如佛以功德智慧。度脱众生入涅盘为事。魔常以破坏众生善根。令流转生死为事。若能安心正道。是故道高方知魔盛。仍须善识魔事。但有四种。一烦恼魔二阴入界魔三死魔。四鬼神魔。三种皆是世间之常事。及随人自心所生。当须自心正除遣之。今不分别鬼神魔相。此事须知。今当略说。鬼神魔有三种。一者精魅。十二时兽变化作种种形

简体字

## 覺知魔事第八

[0470b02] 　　梵音魔羅。秦言殺者。奪行人功德之財。殺行人智慧之命。是故名之為惡魔。事者如佛以功德智慧。度脫眾生入涅槃為事。魔常以破壞眾生善根。令流轉生死為事。若能安心正道。是故道高方知魔盛。仍須善識魔事。但有四種。一煩惱魔二陰入界魔三死魔。四鬼神魔。三種皆是世間之常事。及隨人自心所生。當須自心正除遣之。今不分別鬼神魔相。此事須知。今當略說。鬼神魔有三種。一者精魅。十二時獸變化作種種形

正體字

# CHAPTER EIGHT
## Recognizing the Work of Demons

8. SECTION EIGHT: RECOGNIZING THE WORK OF DEMONS

   a. [FOUR CATEGORIES OF DEMONS]

In Sanskrit, the term is *"māra."* In our language (lit. "the language of the Qin State"), it is rendered as "killer." They plunder the practitioner's merit wealth and slay the wisdom life of the practitioner. Hence, as for that which is referred to as "the work of demons," just as the Buddha takes as his work the use of merit and wisdom to liberate beings that they might enter nirvāṇa, the demons take as their work the continual destruction of beings' roots of goodness that they might be caused to flow along and turn about in the realms of cyclic births and deaths.

If one is able to establish the mind in the right path, it therefore becomes a case of "where the path is lofty, one knows then that the demons will flourish." Hence it is still necessary to be skillful in the recognition of the work of demons.

There are only four categories: First, the affliction demons; second, the demons of the [five] aggregates, [twelve] sense bases, and [eighteen] sense realms; third, the death demons; and fourth, the ghost-and-spirit demons.

   1) [THREE CATEGORIES AS COMMON MENTAL PHENOMENA]

Three of them are normal worldly phenomena as well as products of a given individual's mind. One must get rid of them by rectifying one's own mind, thus exorcising them. We will not describe them in detail just now.

   2) [GHOST-AND-SPIRIT DEMONS]

As for the signs of the ghost-and-spirit demons, these are matters which must be understood. We shall now discuss them briefly. There are three categories of ghost-and-spirit demons: [First, the sprites, goblins, and creatures of the twelve horary time periods; second, *"duiti"* demons; and third, demon-generated afflictions].

   a) [SPRITES, GOBLINS, AND CREATURES OF THE TWELVE HORARY TIME PERIODS]

As for the first, the sprites, goblins, and creatures of the twelve horary time periods, they transform into all sorts of different shapes

色。或作少女老宿之形。乃至可畏身等非一。恼惑行人。此诸精魅欲恼行人。各当其时而来。善须别识若于寅时来者必是虎兽等。若于卯时来者必是兔鹿等。若于辰时来者必是龙鼋等。若于已时来者必是蛇蟒等。若于午时来者必是马驴驼等。若于未时来者必是羊等。若于申时来者必是猿猴等。若于酉时来者必是鸡乌等。若于戌时来者必是狗狼等。若于亥时来者必是猪等。子时来者必是鼠等。丑时来者必是牛等。行者若见常用此时来。即知其兽精。说其名字诃责即当谢灭。二者堆剔鬼。亦作种种恼触行人。或如虫蝎缘人头面。钻刺熠熠或击枥人两腋下。

色。或作少女老宿之形。乃至可畏身等非一。惱惑行人。此諸精魅欲惱行人。各當其時而來。善須別識若於寅時來者必是虎獸等。若於卯時來者必是兔鹿等。若於辰時來者必是龍鼋等。若於已時來者必是蛇蟒等。若於午時來者必是馬驢駝等。若於未時來者必是羊等。若於申時來者必是猿猴等。若於酉時來者必是鷄烏等。若於戌時來者必是狗狼等。若於亥時來者必是猪等。子時來者必是鼠等。丑時來者必是牛等。行者若見常用此時來。即知其獸精。說其名字訶責即當謝滅。二者堆剔鬼。亦作種種惱觸行人。或如蟲蝎緣人頭面。鑽刺熠熠或擊櫪人兩腋下。

正體字

and forms, perhaps taking on the form of a young girl or an old person, or even appearing in fearsome physical forms not limited to any single type. They aggravate and deceive the practitioner. All of these sprites and goblins desire to afflict practitioners. Each of them comes at a time corresponding to its appointed hour. It is necessary to become skillful in distinguishing and recognizing them.

If they come during the *yin* time period (3:00–5:00 A.M.), they are certainly tigers or other such creatures.

If they come during the *mao* period (5:00–7:00 A.M.), they are certainly rabbits, deer, and so forth.

If they come during the *chen* period (7:00–9:00 A.M.), they are certainly dragons, turtles, and so forth.

If they come during the *si* time period (9:00–11:00 A.M.), they are certainly snakes, pythons, and so forth.

If they come during the *wu* period (11:00 A.M. to 1:00 P.M.), they are certainly horses, mules, camels, and so forth.

If they come during the *wei* time period (1:00–3:00 p.m), they are certainly sheep, and so forth.

If they come during the *shen* time period (3:00–5:00 P.M.), they are certainly monkeys, baboons, and so forth.

If they come during the *you* time period (5:00–7:00 P.M.), they are certainly chickens, crows, and so forth.

If they come during the *xu* time period (7:00–9:00 P.M.), they are certainly dogs, wolves, and so forth.

If they come during the *hai* time period (9:00–11:00 P.M.), they are certainly pigs and such.

If they come during the *zi* time period (11:00 p.m. to 1:00 A.M.), they are certainly rats and such.

If they come during the *chou* time period (1:00–3:00 A.M.), they are certainly oxen and such.

If the practitioner observes that they always come at this particular time, he may then know which creature goblin it is. He should then declare its name to scold and rebuke it, whereupon it should retreat and disappear.

b) [*Duiti* Ghosts]

Second, the *duiti* ghosts. They too generate all sorts of aggravating contacts which they inflict upon practitioners. Sometimes they manifest like insects or scorpions which attack a person's head or face, producing a drilling and piercing sensation attended by intense bright light. Sometimes they strike or constrict a person's sides or

或乍抱持于人。或言说音
声喧闹。及作诸兽之形异
相非一。来恼行人。应即
觉知一心闭目阴而骂之作
是言。我今识汝汝是阎浮
提中食火臭香。偷腊吉支
邪。见喜破戒种。我今持
戒终不畏汝。若出家人应
诵戒本。若在家人应诵三
归五戒等。鬼便却行匍匐
而去。如是若作种种留难
恼人相貌。及馀断除之
法。并如禅经中广说。三
者魔恼。是魔多化作三种
五尘境界。相来破善心。
一作违情事则可畏五尘令
人恐惧。二作顺情事则可
爱五尘令人心着。三非违
非顺事。则平等五尘动乱
行者。是故魔名杀者。亦
名华箭。亦名五箭。射人
五情故。

或乍抱持於人。或言說音
聲喧闹。及作諸獸之形異
相非一。來惱行人。應即
覺知一心閉目陰而罵之作
是言。我今識汝汝是閻浮
提中食火臭香。偷臘吉支
邪。見喜破戒種。我今持
戒終不畏汝。若出家人應
誦戒本。若在家人應誦三
歸五戒等。鬼便却行匍匐
而去。如是若作種種留難
惱人相貌。及餘斷除之
法。並如禪經中廣說。三
者魔惱。是魔多化作三種
五塵境界。相來破善心。
一作違情事則可畏五塵令
人恐懼。二作順情事則可
愛五塵令人心著。三非違
非順事。則平等五塵動亂
行者。是故魔名殺者。亦
名華箭。亦名五箭。射人
五情故。

简体字               正體字

perhaps suddenly clutch a person in their embrace, or sometimes they speak, make noises, howl, and even appear in the forms of beasts, not limiting themselves to a single form of appearance.

One should recognize them immediately, single-mindedly close the eyes to block them from view, and then scold them, saying, for example, such words as these: "I now recognize you. You are a *kṛtya* demon[1] from Jambudvīpa, one who feasts on fires and foul-smelling smoke[2] and one who seeks to plunder ordination careers. You are under the sway of deviant views and thus delight in destroying the ranks of the precept-holders. I am now one who upholds the precepts and am one who will never fear you."

If one is a monastic, he should recite the precept texts. If one is a householder, he should recite the three refuges, the five precepts, and so forth. The ghost will then be driven off, being forced to crawl away. All sorts of other such appearances which present difficulties and which aggravate people as well as other techniques for cutting them off and getting rid of them are all as extensively described in the sutras on dhyāna meditation.

c) [DEMON-GENERATED AFFLICTIONS]

Third, afflictions inflicted by demons. Typically, these demons create by transformation three types of phenomenal states within the sphere of the five sense objects, states which they bring forth to demolish the wholesome mind:

In the case of the first type, one which involves the creation of disagreeable phenomena, these appear as fearsome manifestations of the five sense objects which cause a person to be filled with terror.

In the case of the second type, one which involves the creation of agreeable phenomena, these appear as desirable manifestations of the five sense objects which cause a person to become mentally attached.

In the case of the third type, one which involves phenomena that are neither agreeable nor disagreeable, these appear as neutral manifestations of the five sense objects which distract and confuse the practitioner.

On account of such activities as these, the demons are also referred to as "killers," are also referred to as "floral arrows," and are also referred to as "the five arrows." This is on account of their penetrating a person through the five sense faculties.

名色中作种种境界。惑乱行人。作顺情境者。或作父母兄弟。诸佛形像端正男女可爱之境。令人心着。作违情境界者。或作虎狼师子罗刹之形。种种可畏之像。来怖行人。作非违非顺境者。则平常之事。动乱人心令失禅定。故名为魔。或作种种好恶之音声。作种种香臭之气。作种种好恶之味。作种种苦乐境界。来触人身皆是魔事。其相众多。今不具说。举要言之。若作种种五尘。恼乱于人令失善法。起诸烦恼皆是魔军。以能破坏平等佛法。令起贪欲忧愁瞋恚睡眠等。诸障道法。如经偈中说

欲是汝初军　　忧愁为第二
饥渴第三军　　渴爱为第四
睡眠第五军　　怖畏为第六
疑悔第七军　　瞋恚为第八
利养虚称九　　自高慢人十

简体字

名色中作種種境界。惑亂行人。作順情境者。或作父母兄弟。諸佛形像端正男女可愛之境。令人心著。作違情境界者。或作虎狼師子羅刹之形。種種可畏之像。來怖行人。作非違非順境者。則平常之事。動亂人心令失禪定。故名為魔。或作種種好惡之音聲。作種種香臭之氣。作種種好惡之味。作種種苦樂境界。來觸人身皆是魔事。其相眾多。今不具說。舉要言之。若作種種五塵。惱亂於人令失善法。起諸煩惱皆是魔軍。以能破壞平等佛法。令起貪欲憂愁瞋恚睡眠等。諸障道法。如經偈中說

欲是汝初軍　　憂愁為第二
飢渴第三軍　　渴愛為第四
睡眠第五軍　　怖畏為第六
疑悔第七軍　　瞋恚為第八
利養虛稱九　　自高慢人十

正體字

Within [the mental and physical phenomena of] "name-and-form,"[3] they create all sorts of objective states which deceive and confuse the practitioner. In cases where they create agreeable objective states, they may manifest in the form of parents, siblings, buddhas, attractive men or women, or as other desirable phenomena which cause a person to become mentally attached.

In cases where they create disagreeable objective states, they may manifest in the forms of tigers, wolves, lions, or *rākṣasas*, or may manifest in all sorts of other fearsome appearances by means of which they come forth to terrorize the practitioner.

In cases where they create objective states that are neither disagreeable nor agreeable, they may manifest ordinary phenomena which they employ to distract and confuse the mind of the practitioner, thus causing the loss of dhyāna absorption. Hence they are referred to as "demons."

They may also create all sorts of fine or terrible sounds, or may create all sorts of fragrant or stinking smells, or may create all sorts of fine or terrible tastes, or may create all sorts of anguishing or blissful objective states which they bring forth to inflict upon a person's body. These are all the work of demons. Their signs are multifarious. We will not now describe them all.

To bring up and speak of that which is essential, wherever there is the creation of all sorts of phenomena among the five sense objects which aggravate and confuse a person, causing the loss of good dharmas and the arising of afflictions, these are all activities of the demon armies. They are able to employ them to destroy the normal standard for the Buddha's Dharma and to cause the arising of all sorts of path-blocking dharmas such as desire, worry, anger, sleepiness, and so forth. This is as described in a verse from a sutra:

Desire is the foremost of your armies.
Worry is the second.
Hunger and thirst make up the third army.
Craving is the fourth.

Sleepiness is the fifth of your armies.
Fearfulness is the sixth.
Doubt and remorse make up the seventh army.
Anger is the eighth.

Offering and empty praises are the ninth.
Pridefulness and arrogance are the tenth.

如是等众军　压没出家人
我以禅智力　破汝此诸军
得成佛道已　度脱一切人

[0470c28] 行者既觉知魔事即当却之。却法有二。一者修止却之。凡见一切外诸恶魔境。悉知虚诳不忧不怖。亦不取不舍。妄计分别息心寂然彼自当灭。二者修观却之。若见如上所说种种魔境。用止不去即当反观。能见之心不见处所。彼何所恼。如是观时寻当灭謝。若迟迟不去但当正心。勿生惧想不惜躯命。正念不动。知魔界如即佛界如。若魔界如佛界如。一如无二如。如是了知。则魔界无所

如是等眾軍　壓沒出家人
我以禪智力　破汝此諸軍
得成佛道已　度脫一切人

[0470c28] 行者既覺知魔事即當卻之。卻法有二。一者修止卻之。凡見一切外諸惡魔境。悉知虛誑不憂不怖。亦不取不捨。妄計分別息心寂然彼自當滅。二者修觀卻之。若見如上所說種種魔境。用止不去即當反觀。能見之心不見處所。彼何所惱。如是觀時尋當滅謝。若遲遲不去但當正心。勿生懼想不惜軀命。正念不動。知魔界如即佛界如。若魔界如佛界如。一如無二如。如是了知。則魔界無所

简体字　正體字

Numerous armies such as these
Subdue and bury the monastic.

I use the power of dhyāna and wisdom
To smash all of these armies of yours,
And after realizing the Path of buddhahood,
Bring all beings across to liberation.[4]

b.  [DRIVING DEMONS AWAY]

Once the practitioner has recognized the work of demons, he should immediately drive them away. There are two methods for driving them away, as follows.

1)  [THROUGH CALMING]

The first method involves using calming to drive them off. Whenever one observes any of the external evil demon states, knowing that they are false and deceptive, one refrains from becoming either worried or fearful. Neither does one grasp at them or [actively] reject them or commit the error of indulging in making any calculations or mental discriminations with regard to them. By putting the mind to rest and causing it to abide in quiescence, they should naturally disappear on their own accord.

2)  [THROUGH INSIGHT]

The second involves using insight to drive them off. If one observes any of the different kinds of demon states similar to those discussed above and one then finds that, even though one employs calming, they nonetheless do not go away, one should then immediately turn back one's attention and contemplate the observing mind. One does not then perceive that it abides in any location. What then is it that could be afflicted by them?

When one contemplates in this manner, they should soon disappear. If they are slow to respond and thus fail to go away, one should rectify one's own mind and refrain from generating thoughts of terror. One should not even fear for the loss of one's own physical life. One should rectify one's thought so that it does not move. One should recognize that the suchness (*tathatā*) of the demon realm is just the suchness of the buddha realm and [should thus recognize also] that if the suchness of the demon realm and the suchness of the buddha realm are a single suchness, there cannot be two [different] suchnesses.

If one reaches a complete comprehension in this manner, [one will understand that] there is nothing in the demon realm to be

舍。佛界无所取。佛法自当现前。魔境自然消灭。复次若见魔境不谢。不须生忧。若见灭谢亦勿生喜。所以者何。未曾见有人坐禅见魔化作虎狼来食人。亦未曾见魔化作男女来为夫妇。当其幻化。愚人不了。心生惊怖及起贪着。因是心乱失定发狂。自致其患。皆是行人无智受患。非魔所为。若诸魔境恼乱行人。或经年月不去。但当端心正念坚固不惜身命。莫怀忧惧。当诵大乘方等诸经治魔咒。默念诵之。存念三宝。若出禅定亦当诵咒。自防忏悔

捨。佛界無所取。佛法自當現前。魔境自然消滅。復次若見魔境不謝。不須生憂。若見滅謝亦勿生喜。所以者何。未曾見有人坐禪見魔化作虎狼來食人。亦未曾見魔化作男女來為夫婦。當其幻化。愚人不了。心生驚怖及起貪著。因是心亂失定發狂。自致其患。皆是行人無智受患。非魔所為。若諸魔境惱亂行人。或經年月不去。但當端心正念堅固不惜身命。莫懷憂懼。當誦大乘方等諸經治魔呪。默念誦之。存念三寶。若出禪定亦當誦呪。自防懺悔

简体字　　　　　　正體字

relinquished and nothing in the buddha realm to be seized upon. Of its own accord, the Dharma of the Buddha should then naturally manifest before one, whereupon the demon state should naturally dissolve and disappear.

3) [When Demon States Won't Abate]

a) [Limits of a Demon's Powers]

Additionally, if one observes that a demon state does not disappear, one need not give rise to distress. If one observes that it does disappear, one must not become joyful, either. Why is this? We have not yet observed a case of a person sitting in dhyāna absorption who has observed the demon transform into a tiger or a wolf which has then actually come forth and eaten the person. Nor have we yet observed a case of a demon transforming into a man or woman which has actually come forth and acted as a husband or a wife.

b) [Complicit Role of Demon-state "Victims"]

It is through taking on [an indulging] role in a demon's illusory transformations that a foolish person, failing to completely understand, allows his mind to become alarmed or allows it to generate desire-based attachment. Because of this, the mind becomes chaotic, one loses meditative absorption, and one may behave insanely.

One causes one's own calamity. In every case, it is a matter of the practitioner bringing on a calamity through the absence of wisdom. It is not a case of something actually brought about by the demon.

c) [Additional Techniques for Driving Off Demonic States]

i) [Rectification of One's Own Mind]

If demon states occur which aggravate and disturb the practitioner and which don't go away even after months and years have passed, one must simply make one's own mind upright so that the rectitude of one's own thoughts remains solid. One should [be so determined to maintain mental rectitude that he would] not even shrink from risking his own life [to secure that end].[6] One must not be filled with distress or fearfulness.

ii) [Mantras, Repentances, Precept-Recitation, Rectitude, the Good Guru]

One should recite the demon-countering incantations found within the Great Vehicle *vaipulya*[5] sutras. One should recite them silently and abide in mindfulness of the Triple Jewel. Even when one has emerged from dhyāna absorption, one should still recite the incantations as a self-protective measure. One should perform repentances,

惭愧及诵。波罗提木叉。
邪不干正久久自灭。魔事
众多说不可尽。善须识
之。是故初心行人。必须
亲近善知识。为有如此等
难事。是魔入人心能令行
者。心神狂乱。或喜或忧
因是成患致死。或时令得
诸邪禅定智慧。神通陀罗
尼。说法教化人皆信伏后
即坏人出世善事。及破坏
正法。如是等诸异非一说
不可尽。今略示其要。为
令行人于坐禅中。不妄受
诸境界。取要言之若欲遣
邪归正当观诸法实相。善
修止观无邪不破。故释论
云。除诸法实相。其馀一
切皆是魔事。如偈中说

若分别忆想　　即是魔罗网
不动不分别　　是则为法印

惭愧及誦。波羅提木叉。
邪不干正久久自滅。魔事
眾多說不可盡。善須識
之。是故初心行人。必須
親近善知識。為有如此等
難事。是魔入人心能令行
者。心神狂亂。或喜或憂
因是成患致死。或時令得
諸邪禪定智慧。神通陀羅
尼。說法教化人皆信伏後
即壞人出世善事。及破壞
正法。如是等諸異非一說
不可盡。今略示其要。為
令行人於坐禪中。不妄受
諸境界。取要言之若欲遣
邪歸正當觀諸法實相。善
修止觀無邪不破。故釋論
云。除諸法實相。其餘一
切皆是魔事。如偈中說

若分別憶想　　即是魔羅網
不動不分別　　是則為法印

简体字　　　　　　正體字

should maintain a sense of shame and a dread of blame, and should also recite one's *pratimokṣa* codes.[7]

That which is deviant is unable to interfere with whatsoever is orthodox. After a time, it will fade away on its own accord. The work of demons is of many different sorts. A complete discussion of it would be endless. One must be skillful in recognizing it.

Hence the novice practitioner must draw near to a good and knowledgeable spiritual guide specifically because difficult situations such as these may arise.

d) [SUMMARY STATEMENT ON NEGATIVE EFFECTS OF DEMONS]

These demons may enter into a person's mind thus becoming able to cause the practitioner's mind and spirit to become crazy and disturbed, thus producing swings alternating between joy and depression. On account of this, a calamity could occur which might even lead to one's death. At times, they may cause one to gain deviant forms of dhyāna absorption, wisdom, spiritual powers, or *dhāraṇīs*, or they may even cause one to speak Dharma and engage in teaching and conversion of a sort which influences everyone to believe in and submit to him. In the end, one may do damage to other people's wholesome, world-transcending endeavors and one may even engage in activities destructive of right Dharma.

The various strange phenomena of this sort are not of a single type. If one were to describe all of them, they would be endlessly many. We now only briefly explain their essential features for the sake of preventing the practitioner from erroneously indulging mind states arising during dhyāna meditation.

e) [SUMMARY STATEMENT ON DEMONS AND DRIVING THEM OFF]

To speak of it in a way which grasps what is essential, if one desires to drive away the deviant and return to the orthodox, one should contemplate the true character of dharmas. If one skillfully cultivates calming and insight, there is no deviant phenomenon which will not be demolished. Hence the *[Mahāprajñāpāramitā] Upadeśa* states: "Aside from the true character of dharmas, everything else is demonic phenomena."[8] This is as described in a verse:

If one makes discriminations and engages in reflective intellection,
This then is just the net of Māra.
If one remains unmoving and does not indulge discriminations,
This then is the seal of the Dharma.[9]

治病第九

[0471b03]　行者安心修道。或四大有病。因今用观心息鼓击发动本病。或时不能善调适身心息三事。内外有所违犯故有病患。夫坐禅之法若能善用心者。则四百四病自然除差。若用心失所。则四百四病因之发生。是故若自行化他。应当善识病源善知坐中内心治病方法。一旦动病非唯行道有障。则大命虑失。今明治病法。中有二意。一明病发相。二明治病方法。一明病发相者。病发虽复多途略出不过二种。一者四大增损病相。

治病第九

[0471b03]　行者安心修道。或四大有病。因今用觀心息鼓擊發動本病。或時不能善調適身心息三事。內外有所違犯故有病患。夫坐禪之法若能善用心者。則四百四病自然除差。若用心失所。則四百四病因之發生。是故若自行化他。應當善識病源善知坐中內心治病方法。一旦動病非唯行道有障。則大命慮失。今明治病法。中有二意。一明病發相。二明治病方法。一明病發相者。病發雖復多途略出不過二種。一者四大增損病相。

# CHAPTER NINE
## Treatment of Disorders

Once the practitioner has established his resolve to cultivating the Path, disorders associated with the four great elements may manifest. Based on one's present application of the contemplative mind, the breath may be caused to provoke the activation of latent disorders. Sometimes it happens that one is unable to skillfully and appropriately adjust the three factors of body, mind and breath. Due to interferences between the inward and the outward circumstances, pathological troubles may develop.

Now, as for the dharma of sitting in dhyāna absorption, if one is able to skillfully apply the mind, then the four hundred and four kinds of disorders will naturally be cured. If, however, one fails in the correct placement of the mind, then the four hundred and four kinds of disorders may arise on that very account.

For these reasons, whether one is engaged in practice oneself, or whether one is teaching others, one must become skilled in recognizing the causes of disorders. One must know well the methods for employing the inward mind during sitting meditation to treat disorders. If someday one activates a disorder, it may not simply be a matter of developing an obstruction to practice of the Path. It may be that one has to even contemplate the loss of this one great life.

Now, there are two concepts involved in the explanation of the treatment of disorders. First, one explains the signs which arise when disorders manifest. Secondly, one explains the methods employed in the treatment of disorders.

### a. [SIGNS OF DISORDERS]

First, the explanation of the signs which arise when disorders manifest. Although there are many different species of disorders which may manifest, when set forth in brief, they do not go beyond two categories, as follows.

#### 1) [SIGNS RELATED TO THE FOUR GREAT ELEMENTS]

The first are signs of disorders related to the increase or decrease in the four great elements.

若地大增者则肿结沈重身体枯瘠。如是等百一患生。若水大增者。则痰阴胀满食饮不消。腹痛下痢等百一患生。若火大增者。即煎寒壮热。支节皆痛口气大小便痢不通等。百一患生。若风大增者则身体虚悬。战掉疼痛肺闷胀急。呕逆气急如是等。百一患生。故经云。一大不调百一病起。四大不调四百四病。一时俱动。四大病发各有相貌。当于坐时及梦中察之。二者五藏生患之相

若地大增者則腫結沈重身體枯瘠。如是等百一患生。若水大增者。則痰陰脹滿食飲不消。腹痛下痢等百一患生。若火大增者。即煎寒壯熱。支節皆痛口氣大小便痢不通等。百一患生。若風大增者則身體虛懸。戰掉疼痛肺悶脹急。嘔逆氣急如是等。百一患生。故經云。一大不調百一病起。四大不調四百四病。一時俱動。四大病發各有相貌。當於坐時及夢中察之。二者五藏生患之相。

簡体字　　　　　　　　正體字

a) [EARTH-RELATED SIGNS]

If the great element of earth increases [relative to the other elements], then there may be swelling, obstruction, submersion, or heaviness, and the body may become emaciated. One hundred and one maladies of this sort may arise.

b) [WATER-RELATED SIGNS]

If the great element of water increases [relative to the other elements], then there may occur production of the thick or the thin disease-related fluids, edema, and the failure of food and drink to digest properly. Abdominal pain, diarrhea, and any of one hundred and one different types of related maladies may arise.

c) [FIRE-RELATED SIGNS]

If the great element of fire increases [relative to the other elements], then there may be strong fever in which steaming heat alternates with coldness. The joints may all become painful. The respiration, urination, and defecation may not occur with normal ease and any of one hundred and one different types of related maladies may arise.

d) [WIND-RELATED SIGNS]

If the great element of wind increases [relative to the other elements], then the body may feel as if empty and suspended. There may occur quaking and tremors and the experience of intense pain. The lungs may feel as if pressed down or else may feel distended and urgent in their functioning. There may occur nausea and eructation or an intense urgency to the breathing. Any of one hundred and one different types of such related maladies may arise.

e) [SUMMARY STATEMENT ON ELEMENT-RELATED SIGNS]

Hence a scripture states, "When a single great element is out of adjustment, any of one hundred and one disorders may arise. When the four great elements are out of adjustment, any of four hundred and four disorders may be simultaneously activated."[1]

When the disorders associated with the four great elements manifest, each of them possesses a characteristic appearance. One should be watchful for them when one is sitting in meditation and even during one's dreams.

2) [SIGNS RELATED TO THE FIVE CORE ORGANS]

Second, the signs which occur when the five core organs develop maladies.

。从心生患者。身体寒热。及头痛口燥等。心主口故。从肺生患者。身体胀满。四支烦疼心闷鼻塞等。肺主鼻故。从肝生患者。多无喜心忧愁不乐悲思瞋恚。头痛眼暗昏闷等。肝主眼故。从脾生患者。身体面上游风。遍身[病-丙+习]痒疼痛饮食失味等脾主舌故。从肾生患者。咽喉噎塞。腹胀耳聋等。肾主耳故。五藏生病众多各有其相。当于坐时及梦中察之可知。如是四大五藏。病患因起非

從心生患者。身體寒熱。及頭痛口燥等。心主口故。從肺生患者。身體脹滿。四支煩疼心悶鼻塞等。肺主鼻故。從肝生患者。多無喜心憂愁不樂悲思瞋恚。頭痛眼闇昏悶等。肝主眼故。從脾生患者。身體面上遊風。遍身[病-丙+習]痒疼痛飲食失味等脾主舌故。從腎生患者。咽喉噎塞。腹脹耳聾等。腎主耳故。五藏生病眾多各有其相。當於坐時及夢中察之可知。如是四大五藏。病患因起非

简体字　　　　　　　　　　　　　　正體字

a) [HEART-RELATED SIGNS]

In a case where a malady develops from a cause associated with the heart, the body may become either cold or hot and there may be headaches or, on account of the heart's serving as the ruler of the mouth, there may be such symptoms as dryness of the mouth.

b) [LUNG-RELATED SIGNS]

In the case where a malady has developed from a cause associated with the lungs, the body may become edematous, the four limbs may become aggravatingly painful, the heart may become depressed, or, on account of the lungs' serving as the ruler of the nose, there may be such symptoms as nasal congestion.

c) [LIVER-RELATED SIGNS]

In the case where a malady has developed from a cause associated with the liver, there are usually no joyful thoughts. One may be distressed, worried, or unhappy. One may have melancholic thoughts or anger. The head may ache or, on account of the liver serving as the ruler of the eyes, there may occur such symptoms as dimness, blurriness, or dullness of the eyes.

d) [SPLEEN-RELATED SIGNS]

In a case where a malady develops from a cause associated with the spleen, a traveling wind may afflict the body and the face and there may be irritating itching and pain throughout the body. On account of the spleen serving as the ruler of the tongue, there may occur such symptoms as a seeming loss of flavor in food and drink.[2]

e) [KIDNEY-RELATED SIGNS]

In the case where a malady has developed from a cause associated with the kidneys, the throat may be inclined towards feeling choked or obstructed, the abdomen may become distended and, on account of the kidneys serving as the ruler of the ears, there may occur such symptoms as deafness.

f) [SUMMARY STATEMENT ON ORGAN-RELATED SIGNS]

The disorders produced from the five *core* organs are of many different sorts. Each of them presents its own particular signs. One should investigate them when sitting in meditation and even during one's dreams. One may thus be able to understand them.

3) [SUMMARY STATEMENTS ON DISEASE ETIOLOGY]

The causality involved in pathological maladies associated with the four great elements and the five core organs is not limited to

一。病相众多不可具说。行者若欲修止观法门。脱有患生。应当善知因起。此二种病通因内外发动。若外伤寒冷风热。饮食不消而病。从二处发者。当知因外发动若由用心不调。观行违僻。或因定法发时不知取与而致此二处患生。此因内发病相。复次有三种得病因缘不同。一者四大五藏增损得病如前说。二者鬼神所作得病。三者业报得病。如是等病初得即治甚易得差。若经久则病成。身羸病结治之难愈。二明治病方法者。既深知病源起发。当作方法治之。治病之法乃有多途。举要言之。不出止观二种方便。云何用止治病相。

简体字

一。病相眾多不可具說。行者若欲修止觀法門。脫有患生。應當善知因起。此二種病通因內外發動。若外傷寒冷風熱。飲食不消而病。從二處發者。當知因外發動若由用心不調。觀行違僻。或因定法發時不知取與而致此二處患生。此因內發病相。復次有三種得病因緣不同。一者四大五藏增損得病如前說。二者鬼神所作得病。三者業報得病。如是等病初得即治甚易得差。若經久則病成。身羸病結治之難愈。二明治病方法者。既深知病源起發。當作方法治之。治病之法乃有多途。舉要言之。不出止觀二種方便。云何用止治病相。

正體字

a single type. The symptoms are of many different varieties. They cannot be completely described herein. If the practitioner wishes to cultivate the Dharma entryway of calming-and-insight, it may happen that maladies arise. One should become skillful in recognizing their causal bases. These two categories of disorder may both be activated through either internal or external causes.

In a case where there has been injury from external cold, wind, or heat, and it happens also that one's food and drink are not digesting properly so that the disorder has appeared in both of these [element and organ] locations, one should know then that this is an instance of pathological activity instigated by external causes.

In a case where there has been incorrect adjustment in application of the mind, contradictory and unorthodox contemplative practice, or perhaps misunderstanding of appropriateness in the give-and-take required when meditative absorption dharmas manifest, and when it happens consequently that disorders have developed in both of these [element and organ] locations, this is a case of pathological signs instigated by internal causes.

Additionally, there are three different categories of causal bases for becoming afflicted with disorders: The first consists of excesses and deficiencies in the four great elements and five *core* organs as discussed earlier. The second consists of disorders brought on through the actions of ghosts and spirits. The third consists of disorders brought on as a result of karmic retribution.

Disorders such as these are very easily cured if they are treated immediately when first contracted. If they go on for a long time, however, then the pathology becomes established. If the body becomes emaciated and the disorder becomes anchored in place, then, in proceeding with the treatment of it, it may be difficult to bring about a cure.

b. [Treating Disorders]

Second, explaining the methods for treating the disorders. Having deeply understood the origins of a disorder's arising and manifestations, one should implement a method for treating it. The methods employed in the treatment of disorders are of many types. To bring up those which are essential, they do not go beyond the two skillful means of calming and insight.

1) [Treatment through Calming]

How does one use calming to treat symptoms of a disorder?

有师言。但安心止。在病处即能治病。所以者何。心是一期果报之主。譬如王有所至处群贼逬散。次有师言。脐下一寸名忧陀那。此云丹田。若能止心守此不散。经久即多有所治。有师言。常止心足下。莫问行住寝卧即能治病。所以者何。人以四大不调故。多诸疾患此由心识上缘故。令四大不调。若安心在下。四大自然调适众病除矣。有师言。但知诸法空无所有不取病相。寂然止住多有所治。所以者何。由心忆想。鼓作四大故有病生。息心和悦众病即差。故净名经云。何为病本所谓攀缘。云何断攀缘谓心无所得。

简体字

有師言。但安心止。在病處即能治病。所以者何。心是一期果報之主。譬如王有所至處群賊逬散。次有師言。臍下一寸名憂陀那。此云丹田。若能止心守此不散。經久即多有所治。有師言。常止心足下。莫問行住寢臥即能治病。所以者何。人以四大不調故。多諸疾患此由心識上緣故。令四大不調。若安心在下。四大自然調適眾病除矣。有師言。但知諸法空無所有不取病相。寂然止住多有所治。所以者何。由心憶想。鼓作四大故有病生。息心和悅眾病即差。故淨名經云。何為病本所謂攀緣。云何斷攀緣謂心無所得。

正體字

a) [At the Site of the Disorder]

There are masters who say that if one simply establishes the mind in calming at the site of the disorder, one will immediately be able to cure the disorder. Why is this? The mind is the ruler of this [life's] span of karmic-effect retributions. This [healing effect] is comparable to that circumstance wherein, whenever a king goes somewhere, the bands of rebels suddenly scatter.

b) [At the *Udāna* or *Dantian*]

Next, there are masters who say that one inch below the navel is a location known as the *udāna*. This refers to what we know [in Chinese culture] as the *"dantian."*[3] If one is able to bring the mind to a halt and preserve its point of focus at this location such that it does not become scattered, then after one has done this for a long time, in most cases, there will be that which is remedied.

c) [Beneath the Feet]

There are other masters who say that if one constantly anchors the mind's point of attention beneath the feet without regard to whether one is walking, standing, or lying down to sleep, one will be able to cure disorders. Why is this? This is because it is on account of non-regulation of the four great elements that most illnesses occur. This is brought about by the mind's consciousness becoming anchored in a higher position, thus causing the four great elements to become unregulated. If one anchors the mind below, then the four great elements will naturally become appropriately adjusted and the various disorders will be gotten rid of.

d) [Quiescent Abiding in Calming While Realizing Emptiness]

There are masters who state that one need only realize that all dharmas are empty and that nothing whatsoever exists. If one refrains from seizing upon the symptoms of illness while quiescently abiding in calming, then a cure will be brought about in most cases. Why is this? This is because the mind's reflective intellection pumps up the four great elements and instigates the arising of disorders.

If one puts the mind to rest in harmony and happiness, the various disorders will then be cured. Hence the *Vimalakīrti Sutra* states, "What is it that constitutes the origin of disease? It is the so-called 'manipulation of conditions.' ... How does one cut off the manipulation of conditions? It is through what is known as 'the mind's non-apprehension [of the inherent existence of any phenomena].'"[4]

如是种种说用止治病之相非一。故知善修止法能治众病。次明观治病者。有师言。但观心想。用六种气。治病者即是观能治病。何等六种气。一吹。二呼三嘻。四呵。五嘘。六呬。此六种息皆于唇口之中想心。方便转侧而作绵微。而用颂曰

心配属呵肾属吹
脾呼肺呬圣皆知
肝藏热来嘘字至
三焦壅处但言嘻

[0472a04]　有师言。若能善用观想运。作十二种息能治众患。一上息。二下息。三满息。四焦息。五增长息。六灭坏息。七煖息。八冷息。九冲息。十持息。十一和息。十二补息。此十二息皆从观想心生。今略明十二息对治之相。

如是種種說用止治病之相非一。故知善修止法能治眾病。次明觀治病者。有師言。但觀心想。用六種氣。治病者即是觀能治病。何等六種氣。一吹。二呼三嘻。四呵。五噓。六呬。此六種息皆於唇口之中想心。方便轉側而作綿微。而用頌曰

心配屬呵腎屬吹
脾呼肺呬聖皆知
肝藏熱來噓字至
三焦壅處但言嘻

[0472a04]　有師言。若能善用觀想運。作十二種息能治眾患。一上息。二下息。三滿息。四焦息。五增長息。六滅壞息。七煖息。八冷息。九衝息。十持息。十一和息。十二補息。此十二息皆從觀想心生。今略明十二息對治之相。

簡体字　　　　　　　　　　　　正體字

e) [SUMMARY STATEMENT ON "CALMING" AS A MEANS OF TREATMENT]

All such sorts of explanations promoting the use of calming to treat disease symptoms are not of just one single type. Hence one should realize that one is able to treat a multitude of disorders through skillful cultivation of the dharma of calming.

2) [TREATMENT THROUGH VARIOUS {INSIGHT} CONTEMPLATION TECHNIQUES]

Next, the explanation of using [insight-based] contemplations to treat disorders.

a) [EMPLOYING SIX TYPES OF BREATH]

There are masters who state that one need only engage in contemplation utilizing the mind's visualizing thought while also employing six kinds of subtle energetic breath (*qi* = *prāṇa*) to treat disorders. This is just a case of [insight] contemplation being able to treat disorders. What are the six kinds of breath? The first is blowing (*chui*). The second is exhaling (*hu*). The third is mirthful tittering (*xi*). The fourth is puffing (*he*). The fifth is drawn-out breathing (*xu*). The sixth is normal breathing (*si*).[5] These six kinds of breathing are all created within the lips and mouth and are a skillful means employed by the envisioning mind as one turns to the side, utilizing them in a soft and subtle manner. A verse states:

> The heart belongs to "*he*," the kidneys to "*chui*,"
> The spleen to "*hu*," and the lungs to "*si*"—the sages all know this.
> When the liver heats up, the "*xu*" word comes forth.
> Wherever the Triple Warmer is blocked, one need only intone "*xi*."

b) [EMPLOYING TWELVE TYPES OF RESPIRATION]

There are masters who say that if one is skillful in using vizualizing contemplations in implementing twelve different kinds of respiration, one is able to treat a multitude of maladies. The first is "ascending" respiration. The second is "descending" respiration. The third is "filling" respiration. The fourth is "burning" respiration. The fifth is "extended" respiration. The sixth is "demolishing" respiration. The seventh is "warming" respiration. The eighth is "cooling" respiration. The ninth is "forceful" respiration. The tenth is "retaining" respiration. The eleventh is "harmonizing" respiration. The twelfth is "restoring" respiration.

All twelve of these types of respiration arise from the visualizing mind. We now briefly explain the counteractive features of the twelve types of respiration:

上息治沈重。下息治虛懸。滿息治枯瘠。焦息治腫滿。增長息治羸損。滅壞息治增盛。煖息治冷。冷息治熱。衝息治壅塞不通。持息治戰動。和息通治四大不和。補息資補四大衰。善用此息可以遍治眾患。推之可知。有師言。善用假想觀。能治眾病如人患冷。想身中火氣起即能治冷。此如雜阿含經。治病祕法七十二種法中廣說。有師言。但用止觀。檢析身中四大病不可得。心中病不可得眾病自差。如是等種種說。用觀治病。應用不同善得其意皆能治病。當知止觀二法。若人善得其意則無病不治也。但

"Ascending" respiration counteracts sinking and heaviness.
"Descending" respiration counteracts symptoms of feeling as if
    empty and "suspended."
"Filling" respiration counteracts emaciation.
"Burning" respiration counteracts distention.
"Extended" respiration counteracts injury through wasting away.
"Demolishing" respiration counteracts increasing fullness.
"Warming" respiration counteracts coldness.
"Cooling" respiration counteracts heat.
"Forceful" respiration counteracts non-opening obstructions.
"Retaining" respiration counteracts shaking.
"Harmonizing" respiration counteracts four-element deterioration.
"Restoring" respiration fortifies four-element deterioration.

If one is skillful in using these kinds of respiration, one may be able
to treat all of the many varieties of maladies. If one extrapolates
from this, one will be able to comprehend the techniques.

c)  [Through Visualizing Contemplations]

There are masters who say that, if one is skillful in employing visualizing contemplations in the sphere of conventional [reality], one
will be able to treat a multitude of disorders. For instance, if a person is afflicted with coldness, one may visualize the fire energy
arising within the body and then be able to counteract the coldness.
This accords with the *Saṃyukta Āgama Sutra's* extensive discussion
of seventy-two esoteric therapeutic techniques.

d)  [Through Realization of Unfindability]

There are masters who say that one need only employ calming and
insight to carry out investigative analyses within the body so as
to realize that the disorders of the four great elements cannot be
apprehended as existing and the disorders of the mind cannot be
found either. Thus the multitude of disorders will then be cured
of themselves. There are all sorts of explanations such as these
whereby one employs [insight-based] contemplations to treat disorders. Their implementations differ. However, if one well realizes
their meanings, one may in every case be able to treat disorders.

3)  [Summary Discussion on the Treatment of Disorders]

a)  [General Considerations]

One should understand that if one realizes well the meanings inherent in the two techniques of calming and insight, there is no disorder which will not be cured thereby. However, the faculties and

今时人根机浅钝作此观想
多不成就。世不流传。又
不得于此更学气术休粮恐
生异见。金石草木之药。
与病相应亦可服饵。若是
鬼病当用彊心加呪以助治
之。若是业报病。要须修
福忏悔患则消灭。此[1]一
种治病之法。若行人善得
一意即可自行兼他。况复
具足通达。若都不知则病
生无治。非唯废修正法。
亦恐性命有虞。岂可自行
教人。是故欲修止观之
者。必须善解内心治病方
法。其法非一得意在人岂
可传于文耳。复次用心坐
中治病。仍须更兼具十法
无不有益。十法者。一
信。二用三勤。

今時人根機淺鈍作此觀想
多不成就。世不流傳。又
不得於此更學氣術休糧恐
生異見。金石草木之藥。
與病相應亦可服餌。若是
鬼病當用彊心加呪以助治
之。若是業報病。要須修
福懺悔患則消滅。此[1]一
種治病之法。若行人善得
一意即可自行兼他。況復
具足通達。若都不知則病
生無治。非唯廢修正法。
亦恐性命有虞。豈可自行
教人。是故欲修止觀之
者。必須善解內心治病方
法。其法非一得意在人豈
可傳於文耳。復次用心坐
中治病。仍須更兼具十法
無不有益。十法者。一
信。二用三勤。

简体字　　　　　正體字

potential of people of the present age are shallow and dull. When they carry out these envisioning contemplations, they often fail to succeed. Thus these techniques do not circulate widely in the world. As an additional point, one must not go beyond these techniques to pursue the study of energy-manipulation skills or diets requiring desisting from cereal grains. It is feared that one will then develop heterodox views. Mineral and herbal medicines can be useful in the treatment of disease. Hence they may be consumed as well.

If it is a case of a disorder caused by ghosts, one should employ an intensely resolute mind in the application of mantras, using them as a means to assist the treatment. If it is a case of a disorder brought on by karmic retribution, then it is essential to cultivate merit and repentances. The malady will then disappear. In the case of these two[6] types of treatment methods, where a practitioner has had particularly good success with a specific approach, he may practice it himself and also extend its benefits to others as well. How much the more might this be acceptable where one has succeeded in reaching a complete and penetrating realization.

However, if one has no real knowledge of any of this, then when disorders arise, one will not have any means to treat it. Then, not only would this amount to neglectfulness in one's own cultivation of right Dharma, but one fears it might also be a case of someone's very life being in danger. [Under such circumstances], how could one then resort to one's own practice experience as a basis for offering instruction to others?

Therefore, one who wishes to cultivate calming-and-insight must well understand the treatment techniques based in one's own mind. Those techniques are not limited to a single approach. The realization of the concept is something particular to each person. How then could one be able to transmit such matters solely through writing?

b) [Ten Essential Factors in Treatment of Disorders]

Furthermore, when one applies one's mind to the treatment of disorders while engaged in sitting meditation, it is still essential to also include ten dharmas of which there are none which fail to provide benefit. The ten dharmas are:

1. Faith;
2. Utilization;
3. Diligence;

四常住緣中。五別病因法。六方便。七久行。八知取舍。九持护。十识遮障。云何为信。谓信此法必能治病。何为用谓随时常用。何为勤。谓用之专精不息。取得差为度。何为住缘中。谓细心念念依法。而不异缘。何为别病。因起如上所说。何为方便。谓吐纳运心缘想善巧成就。不失其宜。何为久行。谓若用之未即有益。不计日月常习不废。何为知取舍。谓知益即勤有。损即舍之。微细转心调治。何为持护。谓善识异缘触犯。

四常住緣中。五別病因法。六方便。七久行。八知取捨。九持護。十識遮障。云何為信。謂信此法必能治病。何為用謂隨時常用。何為勤。謂用之專精不息。取得差為度。何為住緣中。謂細心念念依法。而不異緣。何為別病。因起如上所說。何為方便。謂吐納運心緣想善巧成就。不失其宜。何為久行。謂若用之未即有益。不計日月常習不廢。何為知取捨。謂知益即勤有。損即捨之。微細轉心調治。何為持護。謂善識異緣觸犯。

4.  Staying constantly focused on the objective condition;
5.  Distinguishing the causality of the disorder;
6.  Skillful means;
7.  Long-enduring practice;
8.  Understanding selection and relinquishing;
9.  Maintaining and guarding [precept observance]; and
10. Recognizing how to block the arising of obstacles.

What is meant by "faith"? This refers to having faith that this technique is certainly capable of curing the particular disorder.

What is meant by "utilization"? This refers to constant utilization no matter what the circumstances may be at the time.

What is meant by "diligence"? This refers to utilization of the technique in a focused, intense, and unceasing manner wherein one takes the achievement of a cure as the measure of accomplishment.

What is meant by "staying focused on the objective condition"? This refers to maintaining a refined mental focus abiding in constant reliance on the particular [treatment] method while not allowing any change in the object of one's attention.

What is meant by "distinguishing the causality of the disorder"? This is as discussed above.

What is meant by "skillful means"? This refers to being skillful and not failing in appropriateness as one perfects subtle energetic meditation work, application of mind, and development of visualizations.

What is meant by "long-enduring practice"? This means that, should one employ a particular technique and yet not gain immediate benefit from it, one nonetheless ignores the passage of days or months, continuing nonetheless to be constant and unfailing in carrying on with the practice.

What is meant by "understanding selection and relinquishment"? This means that, where one becomes aware of benefits in a given technique, one is then diligent, whereas, where one discovers harmfulness in a given technique, one immediately relinquishes it. One is extremely subtle in applying the mind to the task of making adjustments and implementing treatment methods.

What is meant by "maintaining and guarding [precept observance]"? This means that one is skillful in recognizing how different objective conditions carry the potential to involve one in transgressions [against the moral precepts].

何为遮障。谓得益不向外
说未损不生疑谤。若依此
十法所治。必定有効不虚
者也

何為遮障。謂得益不向外
說未損不生疑謗。若依此
十法所治。必定有効不虛
者也

簡体字                                正體字

What is meant by avoiding obstacles? This means that, should one realize some benefits in one's practice, one does not broadcast [such accomplishments] to others, whereas, so long as one hasn't encountered any harm in [a particular treatment technique], one refrains from generating doubts or slanders toward it.

If one relies upon these ten dharmas in the application of treatment methods, one will definitely find them to be efficacious and will not have undertaken them in vain.

| 证果第十 | 證果第十 |
|---|---|
| [0472b15]　　若行者如是修止观时。能了知一切诸法皆由心生。因缘虚假不实故空。以知空故。即不得一切诸法名字相。则体真止也。尔时上不见佛果可求。下不见众生可度。是名从假入空观。亦名二谛观。亦名慧眼。亦名一切智。若住此观即堕声闻辟支佛地。故经云。诸声闻众等自叹言。我等若闻净佛国土。教化众生心不喜乐。所以者何。一切诸法皆悉空寂。无生无灭无大无小无漏无为。如是思惟不生喜乐。当知若见无为入正位者。其人终不能发三菩提心。此即定力多故不见佛性。 | [0472b15]　　若行者如是修止觀時。能了知一切諸法皆由心生。因緣虛假不實故空。以知空故。即不得一切諸法名字相。則體真止也。爾時上不見佛果可求。下不見眾生可度。是名從假入空觀。亦名二諦觀。亦名慧眼。亦名一切智。若住此觀即墮聲聞辟支佛地。故經云。諸聲聞眾等自歎言。我等若聞淨佛國土。教化眾生心不喜樂。所以者何。一切諸法皆悉空寂。無生無滅無大無小無漏無為。如是思惟不生喜樂。當知若見無為入正位者。其人終不能發三菩提心。此即定力多故不見佛性。 |
| 简体字 | 正體字 |

# CHAPTER TEN

## Realization of the Fruits

10. SECTION TEN: REALIZATION OF THE FRUITS

a. [PROVISIONAL CONTEMPLATIONS]

1) [CONTEMPLATION OF ŚRĀVAKA DISCIPLES AND PRATYEKABUDDHAS]

When the practitioner cultivates calming-and-insight in this manner, he may be able to realize that, in every case, all dharmas arise from the mind and, due to the falseness and insubstantiality of causes and conditions, they are empty. Because he realizes that they are empty, he is unable to apprehend any existence in the names and characteristics linked to any dharma. This constitutes the calming achieved through the comprehension of truth.

At such a time, one does not perceive any fruit of buddha-hood above which may be sought after, nor does one perceive any beings below which could be delivered to liberation. This constitutes moving from [contemplation of] conventional [truth] into the contemplation of [the truth of] emptiness. It is also the contemplation of the two truths, is also a function of the wisdom eye, and is also [the basis of] all-knowledge.

If [one commits the error of] taking up residence in this contemplation, one thereby falls down onto the ground of the Śrāvaka Disciples and Pratyekabuddhas.[1] Thus, the [Lotus] Sutra states that the assembly of Śrāvaka Disciples and others sighed to themselves and said, "If we heard of the purification of buddhalands and of the teaching and transforming of beings, our minds were not pleased. Why is this? All dharmas are empty and still. There is in them no production, no destruction, no greatness, no smallness, no outflows, and no conditioning. Having deliberated in this fashion, we did not generate any joy or happiness in it."[2]

One should realize that if one establishes oneself in a perception of the unconditioned and in so doing then enters into the "correct station" (samyaktva-niyāma),[3] such a person will never be able to generate the mind directed toward samyak saṃbodhi.[4] This is a case of a failure to perceive the buddha nature due to excessive emphasis on the power of meditative absorption.

若菩萨为一切众生。成就一切佛法。不应取着无为而自寂灭。尔时应修从空入假观。则当谛观心性虽空缘对之时。亦能出生一切诸法。犹如幻化虽无定实。亦有见闻觉知等相。差别不同。行者如是观时。虽知一切诸法毕竟空寂。能于空中修种种行。如空中种树。亦能分别众生诸根。性欲无量故则说法无量。若能成就无碍辩才。则能利益六道众生。是名方便随缘止。乃是从空入假观。亦名平等观。亦名法眼。亦名道种智。住此观中智慧力多故。虽见佛性而不明了。菩萨虽复成就此二种观。是名方便观门非正观也。故经云前二观为方便道。因是二空观。

简体字

若菩薩為一切眾生。成就一切佛法。不應取著無為而自寂滅。爾時應修從空入假觀。則當諦觀心性雖空緣對之時。亦能出生一切諸法。猶如幻化雖無定實。亦有見聞覺知等相。差別不同。行者如是觀時。雖知一切諸法畢竟空寂。能於空中修種種行。如空中種樹。亦能分別眾生諸根。性欲無量故則說法無量。若能成就無礙辯才。則能利益六道眾生。是名方便隨緣止。乃是從空入假觀。亦名平等觀。亦名法眼。亦名道種智。住此觀中智慧力多故。雖見佛性而不明了。菩薩雖復成就此二種觀。是名方便觀門非正觀也。故經云前二觀為方便道。因是二空觀。

正體字

2) [CONTEMPLATION OF THE BODHISATTVAS]

The bodhisattva perfects all of the dharmas of a buddha for the sake of all beings. He should not seize upon or become attached to the unconditioned, thus bringing himself to enter a state of quiescent cessation. At such a time, one should instead cultivate going from [contemplation of the truth of] emptiness into the contemplation of conventional [truth]. Then, one ought to carefully contemplate and realize that, although the nature of the mind is empty, nonetheless, when one abides in the dual realm of conditions, one is still able to bring forth all dharmas. They are comparable to magically-conjured illusions or supernaturally-generated transformations. Although they are devoid of any fixed reality, there still do exist different characteristic distinctions in the sphere of seeing, hearing, awareness, knowing, and so forth.

When the practitioner contemplates in this manner, although he realizes that all dharmas are ultimately empty and still, he is nonetheless able to cultivate all kinds of practices in the midst of emptiness. It is just as if he were planting a tree in empty space. One is still able to distinguish the faculties of beings and, based on the incalculable number of individual natures and desires, one is then able to proclaim an incalculable number of different dharmas [for their sakes]. If one is able to perfect unobstructed eloquence, then one will be able to benefit the beings of the six destinies.

This constitutes the calming characterized by skillful means adapted to conditions. This then constitutes a moving from [contemplation of the truth of] emptiness into the contemplation of the conventional [truth]. It is also the evenly balanced contemplation, is also the function of the dharma eye, and is also the knowledge of the aspects of the paths (*mārga-ākara-jñatā*).

If one abides in this contemplation, on account of an excessive emphasis on the power of wisdom, although one *does* succeed in perceiving the buddha nature, still, one does not yet arrive at a completely clear comprehension of it. Although the bodhisattva may succeed in perfecting these two kinds of contemplations, this still only constitutes an entryway involving provisional contemplations. It is not the case that it constitutes the correct contemplation.

3) [SUMMARIZING SCRIPTURAL CITATION]

Hence the [*Bodhisattva Necklace Fundamental Practices*] *Sutra*[5] states: "The previous two contemplations are provisional paths. It is because of the contemplation of these two emptinesses[6] that one

得入中道第一义观。双照二谛心心寂灭。自然流入萨婆若海。若菩萨欲于一念中具足一切佛法。应修息二边分别止行于中道正观。云何修正观。若体知心性非真非假。息缘真假之心名之为正。谛观心性非空非假。而不坏空假之法。若能如是照了。则于心性。通达中道圆照二谛。若能于自心见中道二谛。则见一切诸法中道二谛亦不取中道二谛。以决定性不可得故。是名中道正观。如中论偈中说

因缘所生法　我说即是空
亦名为假名　亦名中道义

**[0472c21]**　深寻此偈意。非惟具足分别中观之相。亦是兼明前二种方便观门旨趣。当知中道正观则是佛眼。一切种智。若住此观则定慧力等。了了

简体字

得入中道第一義觀。雙照二諦心心寂滅。自然流入薩婆若海。若菩薩欲於一念中具足一切佛法。應修息二邊分別止行於中道正觀。云何修正觀。若體知心性非真非假。息緣真假之心名之為正。諦觀心性非空非假。而不壞空假之法。若能如是照了。則於心性。通達中道圓照二諦。若能於自心見中道二諦。則見一切諸法中道二諦亦不取中道二諦。以決定性不可得故。是名中道正觀。如中論偈中說

因緣所生法　我說即是空
亦名為假名　亦名中道義

**[0472c21]**　深尋此偈意。非惟具足分別中觀之相。亦是兼明前二種方便觀門旨趣。當知中道正觀則是佛眼。一切種智。若住此觀則定慧力等。了了

正體字

succeeds in entering the contemplation of the primary meaning of the Middle Way. One engages in simultaneous illumination of the two truths, perceives every single thought-moment as quiescent extinction...and one naturally flows on into the sea of *sarvajñatā*."[7]

If a bodhisattva wishes to perfect all of the dharmas of a buddha in a single thought-moment, he should cultivate the calming which distinguishes the two extremes and should carry it out within the correct contemplation of the Middle Way.

b. [CORRECT CONTEMPLATION]
1) [DEFINING CHARACTERISTICS OF CORRECT CONTEMPLATION]

How does one cultivate the correct contemplation? If one completely comprehends that the nature of the mind is neither true nor false, and if one puts to rest the mind which takes truth and falseness as objective conditions, this constitutes correctness.

If one truly contemplates the nature of mind as neither empty nor conventionally existent while still not refuting those dharmas which are either empty or conventionally existent, and if one is able to realize this sort of complete illumination, then in the very nature of mind, one achieves a penetrating understanding of the Middle Way and achieves perfect illumination of the two truths.

If one is able to perceive the Middle Way and the two truths in one's own mind, then one perceives the Middle Way and the two truths in all dharmas, but still does not seize upon either the Middle Way or the two truths. This is because no definite and fixed nature can be found in them. It is this which constitutes the correct contemplation of the Middle Way. This is as set forth in a verse from the *Treatise on the Middle*:

As for all dharmas produced of causes and conditions,
I declare them to be empty.
They are also [mere] conventional designations,
And also [embody] the meaning of the Middle Way.[8]

In deliberating deeply on the intent of this verse, one finds that it not only completely delineates the characteristics of the contemplation of the middle but also simultaneously clarifies the import of the previous two provisional-contemplation gateways. One should realize that the correct contemplation of the Middle Way involves the buddha eye and the knowledge of all modes (*sarva-kāra-jñatā*). If one abides in this contemplation, then the powers of meditative absorption and wisdom are equal, one completely and utterly

见佛性。安住大乘行步平
正。其疾如风。自然流入
萨婆若海。行如来行。入
如来室。着如来衣。坐如
来座则以如来庄严而自庄
严。获得六根清净入佛境
界。于一切法无所染着。
一切佛法皆现在前。成就
念佛三昧。安住首楞严
定。则是普现色身三昧。
普入十方佛土教化众生。
严净一切佛刹。供养十方
诸佛。受持一切诸佛法
藏。具足一切诸行波罗
蜜。悟入大菩萨位。则与
普贤文殊为其等侣。常住
法性身中。则为诸佛称叹
授记。则是庄严兜率陀
天。示现降神母胎出家诣
道场。降魔怨成正觉转法
轮入涅盘。于十方国土究
竟一切佛事。具足真应二
身。则是初发心菩萨也。
华严经中。初发心时便成
正觉。了达诸法真实之
性。所有慧身

简体字

見佛性。安住大乘行步平
正。其疾如風。自然流入
薩婆若海。行如來行。入
如來室。著如來衣。坐如
來座則以如來莊嚴而自莊
嚴。獲得六根清淨入佛境
界。於一切法無所染著。
一切佛法皆現在前。成就
念佛三昧。安住首楞嚴
定。則是普現色身三昧。
普入十方佛土教化眾生。
嚴淨一切佛刹。供養十方
諸佛。受持一切諸佛法
藏。具足一切諸行波羅
蜜。悟入大菩薩位。則與
普賢文殊為其等侶。常住
法性身中。則為諸佛稱歎
授記。則是莊嚴兜率陀
天。示現降神母胎出家詣
道場。降魔怨成正覺轉法
輪入涅槃。於十方國土究
竟一切佛事。具足真應二
身。則是初發心菩薩也。
華嚴經中。初發心時便成
正覺。了達諸法真實之
性。所有慧身

正體字

perceives the buddha nature, and one becomes peacefully established in the Great Vehicle.

2) [CHARACTERISTICS OF THE BODHISATTVA'S POST-RESOLUTION REALIZATIONS]

"His steps are even and correct and his speed is as fleet as the wind."[9]

"One then naturally flows on into the sea of *sarvajñatā*."[10]

"One carries on the practices of the Tathāgata."[11]

"One enters the room of the Tathāgata. One dons the robe of the Tathāgata. One sits in the seat of the Tathāgata."[12]

In this case, one then takes the adornment of the Tathāgata as one's own adornment and succeeds in realizing purification of the six faculties.[13] One enters into the state realized by the Buddha. One has no defiling attachment to any dharma. All of the Buddha's dharmas entirely manifest before one and one perfects the mindfulness-of-the-Buddha samādhi.

One becomes peacefully established in the foremost *Śūraṅgama* meditative absorption. This is the samādhi wherein one manifests form bodies universally. One universally enters all of the buddhalands of the ten directions, teaching and transforming beings. One adorns and purifies all of the buddha *kṣetras*, makes offerings to the Buddhas of the ten directions, receives and maintains the Dharma treasury of all Buddhas, perfects the pāramitās of all practices, awakens to and enters into the station of the great bodhisattvas, and in doing so becomes a companion of Samantabhadra and Mañjuśrī.

Having come to eternally abide in the Dharma-nature body, one is then praised by the Buddhas and given a prediction of buddhahood. One then adorns the Tuṣita Heaven, manifests descent of his spiritual body into the womb of his mother, leaves behind the home life, goes to the site where the Path is realized (*bodhimaṇḍala*), conquers the demon adversaries, realizes the right enlightenment, turns the wheel of Dharma, and then enters nirvāṇa. Throughout the lands of the ten directions, one brings to perfect completion all of the Buddha's endeavors and becomes complete in the two bodies, the true body and the response body. This then is the realization of the bodhisattva who has initially brought forth the resolve.

In the *Floral Adornment Sutra*, it states: "At the very time when one first brings forth the resolve, one then succeeds in achieving the right enlightenment. One gains a completely penetrating

不由他悟。亦云。初发心菩萨。得如来一身作无量身。亦云。初发心菩萨即是佛。涅盘经云。发心毕竟二不别。如是二心前心难。大品经云。须菩提有菩萨摩诃萨。从初发心即坐道场。转正法轮当知则是菩萨为如佛也。法华经中。龙女所献珠为证。如是等经皆明初心具足一切佛法。即是大品经中阿字门。即是法华经中为令众生开佛知见。即是涅盘经中见佛性故住大涅盘。已略说初心菩萨因修止观证果之相。次明后心证果之相。后心所证境界则不可知。今推教所明。终不离止观二法。所以者何。如法华经云。殷勤称叹诸佛智慧则观义。此即约观以明果也。

简体字

不由他悟。亦云。初發心菩薩。得如來一身作無量身。亦云。初發心菩薩即是佛。涅槃經云。發心畢竟二不別。如是二心前心難。大品經云。須菩提有菩薩摩訶薩。從初發心即坐道場。轉正法輪當知則是菩薩為如佛也。法華經中。龍女所獻珠為證。如是等經皆明初心具足一切佛法。即是大品經中阿字門。即是法華經中為令眾生開佛知見。即是涅槃經中見佛性故住大涅槃。已略說初心菩薩因修止觀證果之相。次明後心證果之相。後心所證境界則不可知。今推教所明。終不離止觀二法。所以者何。如法華經云。殷勤稱歎諸佛智慧則觀義。此即約觀以明果也。

正體字

understanding of the true nature of dharmas. The wisdom body one possesses is not awakened to in reliance on others."[14]

It also states: "The bodhisattva who has generated the initial resolve gains the Tathāgata's singular [Dharma] body and the capacity to create an incalculable number of other bodies."[15]

It also states: "The bodhisattva who has generated the initial resolve is the same as a buddha."[16]

The *Nirvāṇa Sutra* states: "The bringing forth of the resolve and the ultimate realization are indistinguishable. Of these two minds, the first of them is [particularly] difficult [to generate]."[17]

The *Mahāprajñāpāramitā Sutra* states: "Subhūti, there are bodhisattvas, *mahāsattvas* who, from the very point of first bringing forth the resolve, immediately proceed to sit at the site where the Path is realized (*bodhimaṇḍala*) where they then proceed to turn the wheel of the right Dharma. One should realize that these are bodhisattvas acting in the same way as buddhas."

In the *Lotus Sutra*, the instance of the jewel being offered up by Dragon Daughter serves as a corroborating case. Sutras such as these all clarify that, in the initial establishment of resolve, one perfects all of the dharmas of the Buddha. This is just as exemplified by the *Mahāprajñāpāramitā Sutra*'s gateway of the syllable "*a*," just as exemplified by the concept in the *Lotus Sutra* of teachings being for the sake of causing beings to open up the knowledge and vision of the Buddhas, and is also just as exemplified by the concept in the *Nirvāṇa Sutra* of abiding in the great nirvāṇa through perceiving the Buddha nature.

We have already explained in brief the initial-resolve bodhisattva's signs of realizing the fruits arising on account of cultivating calming-and-insight.

3) [CHARACTERISTICS OF LATER-STAGE REALIZATIONS]

Next, elucidation of the characteristics of realization of the fruits on the part of later-stage minds. The states of realization which develop for those with later-stage minds are not such as we can cognize. However, if we now extrapolate from what the teachings make clear, we find that they never depart from the two dharmas of calming and insight.

So, how is this the case? Take for example when the *Lotus Sutra* states that [the Buddha] assiduously praised the wisdom of the Buddhas. This is a reference to the concept of [insight] contemplation. This is a case of employing a correlation to [insight] contemplation as a means of elucidating its fruits.

（below）

---

涅盘经。广辩百句解脱以释大涅盘者。涅盘则止义。是约止以明果也。故云。大般涅盘名常寂定。定者即是止义。法华经中。虽约观明果则摄于止。故云。乃至究竟涅盘。常寂灭相终归于空。涅盘中虽约止明果。则摄于观。故以三德为大涅盘。此二大经。虽复文言出没不同。莫不皆约止观二门。辨其究竟并据定慧两法。以明极果。行者当知初中后果。皆不可思议故。新译金光明经云。前际如来不可思议。中际如来种种庄严。后际如来常无破坏。皆约修止观二心。以辨其果。故般舟三昧经中偈云

诸佛从心得解脱
心者清净名无垢
五道鲜洁不受色
有学此者成大道

简体字

涅槃經。廣辯百句解脱以釋大涅槃者。涅槃則止義。是約止以明果也。故云。大般涅槃名常寂定。定者即是止義。法華經中。雖約觀明果則攝於止。故云。乃至究竟涅槃。常寂滅相終歸於空。涅槃中雖約止明果。則攝於觀。故以三德為大涅槃。此二大經。雖復文言出沒不同。莫不皆約止觀二門。辨其究竟並據定慧兩法。以明極果。行者當知初中後果。皆不可思議故。新譯金光明經云。前際如來不可思議。中際如來種種莊嚴。後際如來常無破壞。皆約修止觀二心。以辨其果。故般舟三昧經中偈云

諸佛從心得解脱
心者清淨名無垢
五道鮮潔不受色
有學此者成大道

正體字

As for the *Nirvāṇa Sutra's* expansive description employing a hundred statements on the topic of liberation as a means of explaining the great nirvāṇa, nirvāṇa corresponds to the meaning inherent in calming. This is a case of employing a correlation with calming as a means of elucidating its fruits.

Therefore it states that the great *parinirvāṇa* is an eternal quiescent meditative absorption. As for "meditative absorption," it corresponds to the meaning inherent in calming.

Although in the *Lotus Sutra,* the correlation to [insight] contemplation is employed as a means of elucidating its fruits, it is nonetheless also inclusive of calming. Hence it states, "[The characteristic of liberation, the characteristic of abandonment, the characteristic of cessation], as well as the ultimate nirvāṇa's characteristic of eternal quiescent extinction are all finally returnable to emptiness."[18]

Although in the *Nirvāṇa Sutra,* the correlation to calming is employed to elucidate its fruits, it is nonetheless also inclusive of [insight] contemplation. Hence it takes the three qualities[19] as constituting the great nirvāṇa.

Although there are differences in the texts of these two great sutras as regards the explicit and the esoteric, it is never the case that they depart from a relationship to the two entryways of calming and insight. In the articulation of their ultimate concepts, they both rely upon the two dharmas of meditative absorption and wisdom in order to elucidate the utmost fruits [of cultivating the path] The practitioner should realize that the initial, middle and later fruits are all inconceivable and ineffable. Hence the new translation of the *Golden Light Sutra* states, "The Tathāgatas at the beginning are inconceivable and ineffable. The Tathāgatas during the intermediate phase engage in all sorts of adornments [of the Dharma realm of beings and in every case it is for the sake of benefiting others.] The Tathāgatas at the final phase are eternally indestructible."[20]

In every case the correlation to the cultivation of the two minds of calming and insight is employed to articulate the fruits [of cultivation]. Hence a verse from the *Pratyutpanna Samādhi Sutra* states:

It is from the mind that all buddhas gain liberation.
As for the mind, it is pure and known as undefiled.
Even in the five destinies, it remains fresh and immaculate and
takes on no form.
Where there is one who studies this, he perfects the great Path.[21]

[0473b07]　　誓愿所行者须除
三障五盖。如或不除虽勤
用功终无所益

修习止观坐禅法要(终)

[0473b07]　　誓願所行者須除
三障五蓋。如或不除雖勤
用功終無所益

修習止觀坐禪法要(終)

简体字　　　　　　　　　　　　正體字

c. [THE ESSENTIAL PREREQUISITES FOR SUCCESS]

I declare as a matter of solemn oath that, as for that which is practiced, it is essential to get rid of the three obstacles[22] and the five hindrances.[23] In the event that they are not gotten rid of, even though one might be diligent in applying one's efforts, one will ultimately gain no benefit from it.

End of *The Essentials for Practicing Calming-and-Insight and Dhyāna Meditation*

# ENDNOTES

## Preface

1. *Ekottara-āgama-sūtra* (增壹阿含經 – T02.125.551a).
2. Although "fetters" does have technical meanings, it is a general term of reference for afflictions (*kleśa*) such as desire, hatred, and delusion. Fetters are referred to as such because they provoke unwholesome karma which binds one to unenlightened cyclic existence. A more detailed list speaks of the nine fetters: desire, hatred, arrogance, ignorance-generated delusion, doubtfulness, views, grasping (at views), jealousy, stinginess.
3. T09.262.8a.
4. Unable to find the origin of this citation.
5. *Mahā-parinirvāṇa-sūtra* (大般涅槃經 – T12.374.547a).

## Chapter One

1.  *Sutra on the General Teachings and Remonstrances of the Buddha Prior to Parinirvāṇa*, translated by Kumārajīva (佛垂般涅槃略說教誡經 – T12.389.1111a). A "bhikshu," by the way, is a fully ordained celibate-tradition Buddhist monk.

2.  The five "relentless" transgressions are patricide, matricide, killing an arhat, spilling the blood of a Buddha, and causing a schism in the harmoniously-united monastic Sangha. The Sanskrit term connotes immediacy, unavoidability, and relentlessness of hell-bound retribution. These transgressions are discussed in the fourth chapter of the *Abhidharma-kośa-bhāṣyam*.

3.  佛說佛名經 (T14.441.225b, 284b), 大方廣十輪經 (T13.410.709a).

4.  "Sense of shame" (*hrī*) and "dread of blame" (*apatrāpya*) are considered to be "good dharmas" which are included as such in the dharmic-analysis schemas of all traditional Buddhist schools of both Southern and Northern traditions. They are, for instance, contained in the 100 dharmas of Vasubandhu, and in a subset of that schema commonly studied in certain schools of Tibetan Buddhism as "the fifty-one mental factors").

    A sense of shame instills a sensitivity to one's own highest standards of behavior whereas dread of blame instills a sensitivity to the highest behavioral standards of one's peers. They are not intended to produce a mental state eternally freighted with guilt. On the contrary: Where one nourishes these sensitivities, one is bound to avoid negative karma and the guilt which naturally follows in its wake.

5.  I was unable to locate this scripture in the Chinese canon.

6.  Dhyāna Master Baojing notes that this refers to Shakyamuni Buddha's period of cultivating ascetic practices in the Himalayas in this lifetime and also to his cultivation in the mountains in previous lives while coursing along the Bodhisattva Path (p. 53).

7.  "*Dhūta* practices" refers to a dozen ascetic practices which were encouraged by the Buddha for those practitioners who could benefit from them. They included such practices as eating but a single meal each day, sitting up while sleeping at night, etc. They tend to reinforce certain crucial aspects of intense spiritual cultivation and are to be distinguished from the non-beneficial ascetic practices which the Buddha specifically discouraged (such as lying down on a bed of nails, covering oneself with ashes, etc.).

8.  Verbal purification refers to a mental contemplation attended by a verbal statement wherein a monastic offers material goods in excess of one's most basic needs to the Triple Jewel (Buddha, Dharma, and

monastic Sangha), requesting that they compassionately accept their ownership. One then becomes able to use them without the assumption that they belong specifically to one's self. The practical utility of this practice is that it tends to discourage attachment to personal material possessions.

9. According to Śāriputra's classic explanation narrated by Nāgārjuna in fascicle three of *Mahā-prajñāpāramitā-upadeśa* (T25.1509.79c2–80a1), "upwardly" refers to such professions as meteorological and astronomical prognostications, "inferiorly" refers to the blending of herbs, tilling the soil, planting fruit trees and so forth, "midpoints" refers to occult professions involving mantras, oracles, omens and so forth, and "directions" refers to manipulation and flattery of the rich and powerful through activities performed in all four directions intended to obtain their favors. The entire story, as translated in my *Marvelous Stories of the Perfection of Wisdom*:

### Śāriputra Explains Pure Sustenance to Śucimukhī

Śāriputra went into the city to make his alms rounds and, having obtained his food, sat down facing a wall to eat. At this time, a *brahmacarinī* name Śucimukhī came along and saw Śāriputra and asked Śāriputra, "Śramaṇa, are you eating?"

He replied, "Yes, I'm eating."

Śucimukhī asked, "Do you *śramaṇas* eat with your attention directed downwards?"

He replied, "No, Sister."

"Do you eat with your attention directed upwards?"

"No."

"With your attention directed to the [four] directions?"

"No."

"With your attention directed to the four intermediary points?"

"No."

Śucimukhī said, "There are four methods employed in eating. I asked you about them and you said 'no' in every case. I don't understand. You ought to explain."

Śāriputra said, "There are those who have left the home life who blend herbs, sow grains, plant trees, or engage in other such forms of impure means of sustaining one's life. These methods are referred to as "sustenance gained with one's attention directed downwards."

"There are those who have left the home life who observe the stars, the constellations, the sun, the moon, the wind, the rain, thunder and lightning, and lightning bolts, these impure means of sustaining one's life. These methods are referred to as "sustenance gained with one's attention directed upwards."

"There are those who have left the home life who manipulate and flatter the noble and powerful, who deliver messages for them in all four directions, or who employ clever words and covetousness, these impure means of sustaining one's life. These methods are referred to as "sustenance gained with one's attention directed in all directions."

"There are those who have left the home life who study all manner of incantational techniques, or who practice divination and calculation of auspiciousness and inauspiciousness and all kinds of other impure means of sustaining one's life such as these. These methods are referred to as "sustenance gained with one's attention directed on the intermediary points." Sister, I do not fall into any of these four types of impure means of sustaining one's life. I employ the pure alms round to sustain this life."

At this time, when Śucimukhī had heard the explanation of the dharma of pure sustenance, she was delighted and developed faith and understanding. On account of having spoken Dharma for her, Śāriputra gained the way of the *srota-āpanna* (first-stage arhat).

10. An *araṇya* is a quiet meditation hermitage. As for the Chinese unit of distance measure, there are roughly three Chinese *li* in a mile.

## Chapter Two

1. Nāgārjuna, from *Mahā-prajñāpāramitā-upadeśa* (T25.1509.181b–c), as translated in *Nāgārjuna on the Six Perfections*:

   How does one renounce sounds? It is the characteristic of sounds that they do not abide. One hears them only momentarily and then they immediately disappear. Because foolish people do not understand a sound's characteristic of being impermanent and disappearing, they erroneously develop fondness and pleasure in relation to sounds. They retain in their minds sounds which have already passed and bring forth attachment to them.

   This is illustrated by the case of the five hundred rishis who dwelt in the mountains. A *kinnara* maiden was bathing in a pool in the Snow Mountains. When they heard the sound of her singing, they immediately lost their dhyāna absorptions. Their minds became drunken, crazed, and so unrestrained that they were unable to control themselves. It was as if a great gale had begun to blow through the trees in the forest. When they heard this subtle and marvelous singing voice which was so soft and pure, they brought forth aberrant thoughts. On account of this, without their even being aware of it, their minds became deranged.

   Thus it is that one may lose one's meritorious qualities in the present life and even become bound in later lives to fall into the wretched destinies.

   A person possessed of wisdom contemplates sounds and perceives that, in every new thought-moment, they are produced and destroyed, that the prior and latter sounds do not include each other, and that they are not continuous. If one is able to develop an understanding such as this, then one does not bring forth defiling attachments. Whosoever is a person like this is unable to become disoriented even by the music of the gods, how much the less by the voices of humans. All sorts of causes and conditions such as these serve to illustrate what is meant by renouncing the desire for sounds.

2. "Fetters" (*saṃyojana*) are just the afflictions of greed, hatred, stupidity, arrogance, doubt, etc. which tie people up and bind them to the world.

3. Nāgārjuna, from *Mahā-prajñāpāramitā-upadeśa* (T25.1509.181c–2a), as translated in *Nāgārjuna on the Six Perfections*:

   Additionally, there was a bhikshu who was walking next to a lotus pool in the forest. When he smelled the fragrance of the lotus blossoms, his mind was pleased and so experienced a feeling of pleasure. Having passed on by, his mind engendered a fondness for it.

   The pond spirit then spoke to him, saying, "Why is it that you have forsaken that place beneath the trees wherein you have been sitting purely in dhyāna meditation and have now come forth to steal these fragrances of mine? It is on account of attachment to fragrances that dormant fetters may be caused to arise."

At that time, yet another person came along who entered right into the pool and took many of its flowers. He proceeded to dig, pulled forth roots and stems, created a disorderly mess, and then left. The pond spirit remained silent and did not say anything at all.

The Bhikshu then said, "This person destroyed your pond and took your flowers. You didn't say anything whatsoever to him. However, I merely passed by the bank of the pond and then suffered your rebuke and a scolding in which you claimed that I had stolen your fragrances."

The pond spirit said, "The evil people of the world are always immersing their heads in the excrement of offense-related defilement. I do not even bother to speak to them. You, however, are a fine person who engages in the practice of dhyāna meditation. Thus, when you become attached to these fragrances, it destroys your fine endeavors. It is for this reason that I scolded you."

This is analogous to a white cloth which is fresh and pure but then gets a spot where it has become stained by something black. Everyone sees it. In the case of those who are evil persons, it is analogous to an already black robe becoming spotted with ink. It is such as people would not even notice. So, who would even bring it up?

All sorts of causes and conditions such as this constitute what is meant by renouncing the desire for fragrances.

4.  Nāgārjuna, from *Mahā-prajñāpāramitā-upadeśa* (T25.1509.182a), as translated in *Nāgārjuna on the Six Perfections*:

    What is meant by renouncing tastes? One ought to make oneself aware that, "Solely on account of desirous attachment to fine flavors, I may become bound to undergo a multitude of sufferings wherein molten copper is poured down the mouth and I am forced to consume burning hot iron pellets."

    If one fails to observe the Dharma in its applications to eating, and if one's thoughts of particular fondness become solidly attached, one may fall down amongst the worms who course in the midst of impurities. This is exemplified by the one *śrāmaṇera* whose mind became constantly fond of curds. Whenever the *dānapatis* made a food offering to the Sangha of curds, the portion which was left over would always be passed on to that *śrāmaṇera*. In his thoughts, he became lovingly attached to it, taking such pleasure and delight that he was unable to separate from it. After the end of his life he was reborn in this vase of leftover curds. The master of that *śrāmaṇera* had gained the way of arhatship. When the Sangha divided up the curds, he said to them, "Be careful, be careful. Don't injure the curd-loving śrāmaṇera."

Everyone said, "But this is just a worm. Why do you refer to it as 'the curd-loving śrāmaṇera'?"

He replied, saying, "Originally, this worm was my śrāmaṇera. Because he only sat there engaged in a gluttonous affection for leftover curds, he came to be reborn in this vase. When the master received his share of the curds, the worm came along within it. The master said, "Curd-loving fellow. Why did you come here?" He then gave it the curds.

5.   Nāgārjuna, from *Mahā-prajñāpāramitā-upadeśa* (T25.1509.183a–c), as translated in *Nāgārjuna on the Six Perfections*:

In a time long ago and far off in the past there was a rishi in the mountains of the state of Benares who, in the early spring was relieving himself into a wash basin when he observed a buck and a doe mating. Lustful thoughts suddenly arose in him, whereupon his semen flowed into the basin.

The doe happened to drink from that basin and then became pregnant. When the months of pregnancy were complete, she gave birth to a fawn with the appearance of a man. There was only one horn on the head and his feet were like that of deer. When the deer was about to give birth, she went to a place alongside the rishi's hut and then gave birth. She saw that her fawn was a person and so entrusted it to the rishi and left.

When the rishi came out, he saw this progeny of the deer, recalled to himself the original conditions, knew that it was his own son, and so took him and raised him. As the son grew to adulthood, he diligently instructed him in the topics of study so that he was able to gain a penetrating understanding of the eighteen great classics. Additionally, he studied sitting in dhyāna, practiced the four immeasurable minds, and then immediately gained the five superknowledges.

Once, he was climbing up the mountain and encountered a great rainstorm. The mud became so slippery that he lost his footing, fell to the ground, broke his ewer and injured his foot. He then became greatly enraged. Because his ewer had been full of water, he cast a spell which caused it to not rain any more. On account of the meritorious qualities possessed by this rishi, the dragons, ghosts and spirits all saw to it that it did not rain.

Because it did not rain, the five types of grains and the five types of fruit all failed to grow. The populace became impoverished, destitute, and bereft of any means to survive. The king of the state of Benares was distressed, worried, and tormented by grief. He ordered all of the great officials to convene and discuss the rainfall situation.

One of the wise ones among them offered an opinion, saying, "I have heard it rumored that there is a one-horned rishi up in the Rishi Mountains who, on account of losing his footing, fell down and injured his foot as he was climbing the mountain. In a fit of anger, he cast a spell on these rains and thus caused them to not fall at all for the ensuing twelve years."

The King thought to himself, "If it goes twelve years without raining, my country will surely be finished. There will be no people left at all." The King then issued an appeal, stating, "Could it be that there is someone who, for the sake of the population, will be able to instruct me in how to cause a rishi to lose his five superknowledges? If so, I will divide the country with them so that we might each rule over half of it."

In this country of Benares, there was a courtesan by the name of Śāntā who was incomparably beautiful. She came in response to the King's appeal and asked everyone there, "Is this individual a man or not?"

Everyone replied, "He is a man, that's all. He was born to a rishi."

The Courtesan said, "If he is a man, I will be able to destroy him." After she had said this, she took up a gold tray filled with fine and precious things, and told the King, "I will come back here mounted on the neck of this rishi."

The Courtesan then immediately sought to assemble five hundred carriages carrying five hundred beautiful maidens and five hundred deer-carts carrying all sorts of delightful morsels all of which had been admixed with many herbs. She used many different hues to color them so that they appeared like various kinds of fruits and then took all sorts of greatly powerful fine liquors which, in appearance and flavor, were identical to water.

They dressed in tree bark clothing and grass clothing and traveled into the forest, appearing thereby as if they were rishis themselves. They set up grass huts off to the side of the Rishi's hut and then took up residence there. The one-horned Rishi was wandering about and observed them. The maidens all came out and welcomed him. They used beautiful flowers and fine incenses as offerings to the Rishi. The Rishi was greatly delighted.

All of the maidens used lovely words and respectful phrases in greeting the Rishi. They took him on into their quarters and sat with him on fine bedding. They gave him fine clear liquor which he took to be pure water. They gave him delightful morsels which he took to be fruit. After he had feasted and drunk his fill, he told the maidens, "From the time of my birth on up to the present, this is a first. I have never yet had such fine fruit and such fine water."

The maidens said, "It is because we have been single-minded in our practice of goodness that the gods fulfill our wishes to obtain these fine fruits and fine water."

The Rishi asked the maidens, "How is it that your complexions and bodies are so full and flourishing?"

They replied, saying, "It is because we eat these fine fruits and drink this marvelous water that our bodies are so full and flourishing as this." The maidens asked the Rishi, "Why don't you come and live here among us?"

He replied, "I, too, could abide here."

The maidens said, "We could bathe together." He then assented to that as well. The hands of the maidens were soft and tender. When they touched him, his mind moved. He then continued to bathe together with the beautiful maidens. Desirous thoughts arose and consequently he engaged in sexual intercourse. He immediately lost his superknowledges, whereupon the heavens made a great downpour of rain which went on for seven days and seven nights, allowing them the opportunity to continue engaging together in the delights of food and drink.

After the seven days had passed, the liquor and fruit were all gone, whereupon they continued to supply their needs with the waters of the mountain and the fruits from the trees. However, their flavors were not so marvelous, and so he sought more of what they had enjoyed before.

She responded by saying, "Those things are already used up. We must now go together to a place, not far from here, where more of them may be obtained."

The Rishi said, "We can do as you wish." They then went off together. The Courtesan knew when they had come to a spot not far from the city. The maiden then lay down in the middle of the road and said, "I'm exhausted. I can't walk any further."

The Rishi said, "If it's the case that you cannot walk, sit up on my shoulders and I will carry you forth."

The maiden had already sent a letter on ahead to the King in which she told the King, "The King will be able to observe my intelligence and abilities."

The King ordered up his official carriage and went forth to observe them. He asked, "How did you manage to bring this about?"

The maiden addressed the King, saying, "It is on account of the power of skillful means that I have now caused the situation to develop in this way. I have no abilities beyond this. Order him to live within the city. Make fine offerings to him and pay respects to him. Keep him satisfied with the five objects of desire."

The King honored him with the status of a great official. He had dwelt in the city for only a short span of days when his body became haggard and emaciated. He remembered the mental bliss of dhyāna absorptions and so grew disgusted with these worldly desires. The King asked the Rishi, "How is it that you have become so unhappy that your body is now so haggard and emaciated?"

The Rishi replied to the King, "Although I have gained the five desires, I constantly recall to mind the leisure and stillness in the forest, the wandering place of all the rishis. I cannot get it out of my mind."

The King thought to himself, "If I force him to go against his aspirations, such a going against one's aspirations is suffering. If the suffering reaches an extreme, he will die. Originally, this was done out of a desire to get rid of the calamity of drought. Now that I have already succeeded in that, why should I continue to forcibly keep him from his aspirations?"

And so it was that he was released straightaway. After he returned to the mountains, he had not applied himself vigorously for long before he gained the five superknowledges once again.

6.  Zhiyi's alternate Sino-Buddhist title for Nāgārjuna's *Mahā-prajñāpāramitā-upadeśa*.

7.  *Mahā-prajñāpāramitā-upadeśa* (T25.1509.181a). Although presented as a unitary quotation, this is actually a series of unconnected quotes, with minor textual variations.

8.  治禪病祕要法 (T15.620.336c).

## Chapter Three

1.  *Āvaraṇa*, one of two alternate Sanskrit antecedents for what are commonly translated into English as the five "hindrances" or "obstacles" (the other is *nīvaraṇa*), has a primary meaning of "covering" in addition to its "hindrance"-related meanings. Because many classic-era Sino-Buddhist translations render this "covering" meaning directly, it is in this sense that a number of Zhiyi's hindrance-related comments are framed. Even so, for the sake of easy resonance with other classic discussions on this topic, I have translated the technical term as "hindrance" throughout whilst still preserving this author's specific "covering"-associated comments.

2.  This is a reference to a story related by Nāgārjuna in *Mahā-prajñāpāramitā-upadeśa* (T25.1509.166a–b). It does require, for maximum effect, that the reader adopt some degree of sympathy with the hierarchical concerns of a caste-based society. It follows here as I have rendered it in both *Nāgārjuna on the Six Perfections* and *Marvelous Stories from the Perfection of Wisdom*:

    There once was a king who had a daughter named Kumuda. There was a fisherman named Śubhakara. He was walking along the road when he looked from afar and saw the princess's face in the window of a tall building. In his imagination, he developed thoughts of defiling attachment which he could not relinquish for even a moment. He went through days and months during which he was unable to drink or eat. His mother asked him the reason and he revealed his feelings to his mother, "I saw the daughter of the King. My mind is unable to forget her."

    The mother explained to her son, "You are a man of lesser station. The daughter of the King is an honored member of the nobility. She is unobtainable."

    The son said, "My mind prays for this bliss and is unable to forget it for even a moment. If I cannot have it as I will it, then I will be unable to go on living."

    For the sake of her son, the mother entered the palace of the King, constantly providing gifts of fat fish and fine meats which she left for the daughter of the King without asking any remuneration. The princess thought this strange and so asked her what wish she was seeking to fulfill.

    The mother addressed the princess, "Pray, dismiss the retainers. I must relate a personal matter." [She then continued], "I have only one son. He cherishes a respectful admiration for the daughter of the King. His feelings have taken hold in a way that has caused him to become ill. He is not likely to survive much longer. I pray that you will condescend to have pity on him and give him back his life."

The princess said, "On the fifteenth of the month have him go into such-and-such a deity's shrine and stand behind the image of the deity."

The mother returned and told her son, "Your wish has already been fulfilled." She then described what had transpired. He bathed, put on new clothes, and stood behind the image of the deity.

When the time came, the princess told her father, the King, "I have something inauspicious which has come up. I must go to the shrine of the deity and seek for auspiciousness and blessings."

The King replied, "That is very good." He then had five hundred carriages adorned which then proceeded to the shrine of the deity. Having arrived, she ordered her retainers to close the doors and wait as she entered the shrine alone.

The heavenly spirit thought, "This should not be this way. The King is the lord of the land. I cannot allow this petty man to destroy and dishonor the princess." He then caused the man to become tired and to fall into a sleep from which he did not awaken.

Having entered, the princess saw him sleeping. She shook him very hard and yet he did not awaken. She left him a necklace worth a hundred thousand ounces of gold and then went away.

After she had left, this man was able to awaken and see that the necklace was there. Next, he asked a person in the crowd. He then knew that the King's daughter had come. Because he was unable to follow up on his infatuation, he became distressed, full of regret, and overcome with the affliction of grief. The fire of lust broke loose within him. He was burned up by it, and then died.

3.  Nāgārjuna devotes considerable energy to emphasizing the negative points of desire as a hindrance to acquisition of meditative absorption. I quote here a section from his discussion of the five hindrances wherein he presents some forty analogies on this topic, this from *Nāgārjuna on the Six Perfections* (T25.1509.185a–b):

Moreover, one seeks exclusively to gain the first dhyāna and, in doing so, renounces the pleasures of desire. By way of analogy, it is as if one were to constantly strive to exterminate an enemy who threatens one with calamity, this so that one cannot be injured by that enemy.

This is illustrated by what the Buddha said to the Brahman who was attached to desire: "I originally contemplated desire and realized that desire constitutes a cause and condition for apprehensiveness, distress, and suffering. Desire brings only few pleasures, whereas its sufferings are extremely numerous."

Desire is the net of the demons and an entangling web from which it is difficult to escape. Desire constitutes a burning heat which dries up all bliss. It is like being in a forest with fire rising up on all four sides. Desire, like drawing close to a fiery pit, is extremely fearsome. It is like cornering a venomous snake, like an enemy invader brandishing a knife, like an evil rākṣasa ghost, like deadly poison entering the mouth, like swallowing molten copper, like three columns of crazed elephants, like drawing close to an extremely deep abyss, like a lion blocking one's path, like the Makara fish-monster opening its maw. All of the desires are just like this and are very much worthy of being feared. The desires cause people to undergo torment and suffering.

Those people who are attached to desire are like convicts in a prison, like deer caught in a corral-trap, like birds snared in a net, like fish who have swallowed a hook, like a dog pounced upon by a leopard, like a crow in the midst of a band of owls, like a snake which has run up against a wild boar, and like a mouse among cats. They are like blind men approaching an abyss, like a fly caught in hot oil, like a peaceful man caught up in military combat, like a lame person who has entered a conflagration, like one who has entered a river of boiling brine, like one who licks a honey-smeared blade, and like one [sentenced to be] sliced to ribbons in the city square.

The desires are like a thinly covered grove of knives, like flowers covering filth, like a jar of honey mixed with poison, and like a basket of venomous snakes. They are like the falseness and deception of a dream, like a debt which must be repaid, and like a conjuration which deceives a small child. In their lack of substantiality, they are like the flames of a fire. [Involvement with them] is like being drowned in a great body of water and like when a boat enters into the gullet of the Makara fish-monster.

They are like a hailstorm destroying crops, like crashing thunder and lightning striking right next to a person. The desires are just like this. They are false, deceptive, devoid of substantiality, devoid of durability, devoid of potency, possessing only few pleasures, but many sufferings. The desires constitute an army of demons smashing all of one's goodness and merit.

It is because they constantly serve to plunder and injure beings that we present all sorts of analogies such as these. If one renounces the five desires, gets rid of the five hindrances, and practices the five dharmas, one may then succeed in reaching the first dhyāna.

4.  "Three wretched destinies" refers to three extremely unfortunate realms of rebirth: in the hells, as a hungry ghost, and as an animal.

5.  An incomplete quotation from Nāgārjuna in *Mahā-prajñāpāramitā-upadeśa* (T25.1509.167a). The complete passage as translated in *Nāgārjuna on the Six Perfections* (in the midst of an marvelous discussion of

antidotes to anger):

What thing is it which, killed, brings peace and security?
What thing is it which, if slain, one has no regrets?
What thing is it which is the root of venomousness?
And which devours and destroys all forms of goodness?
What thing is it which one slays and then one is praised?
What thing is it which, slain, brings on no more distress?

The Buddha replied with a verse in which he said:

If one kills anger (*krodha*), the mind will be peaceful and secure.
If one slays anger, the mind will have no regrets.
It is anger which is the root of venomousness.
It is anger which destroys all forms of goodness.
If one slays anger, all buddhas offer praise.
If one slays anger, one has no more distress.

6.  On the question of why "lethargy-and-sleepiness" is a dual-compo-
    nent hindrance, Vasubandhu indicates (in Chapter Five of his *Treasury
    of Analytic Knowledge*) that it is because both "lethargy" and "sleepi-
    ness" are nourished by the same five factors (bad omens seen in
    dreams [*tandrī*]; unhappiness [*arati*]; physical exhaustion [*vijṛmbhikā*];
    uneven consumption of food [*bhakte'samatā*]; mental depression [*cetaso
    līnatva*]), are starved by the same single factor (illuminated perception
    [*āloka-saṃjñā*]), and are productive of the same result of mental lan-
    guor. See Leo Pruden's *Abhidharma-kośa-bhāṣyam* (851–2).

7.  I have reinserted in brackets the couplet missing from this verse
    which Zhiyi otherwise quotes in full from *Mahā-prajñāpāramitā-
    upadeśa* (T25.1509.184b–c). The corresponding Chinese text: 一切世間
    死火燒。汝當求出安可眠。

8.  The "dhyāna wake-up device" refers to a piece of wood connected by
    a string to one's ear which falls and tugs at the ear when the medita-
    tor's posture slumps due to drowsiness.

9.  On the question of why "excitedness-and-regretfulness" is a dual-
    component hindrance, Vasubandhu indicates (in Chapter Five of his
    *Treasury of Analytic Knowledge*) that it is because both "excitedness"
    and "regretfulness" are nourished by the same four factors, namely
    ideation regarding relatives (*jñāti-vitarka*), land (*janapada-vitarka*),
    immortals (*amara-vitarka*), previous pleasures and the associated com-
    panions, are countered by the same single factor (calmness), and are
    productive of the same result of mental agitation. See Leo Pruden's
    *Abhidharma-kośa-bhāṣyam* (852).

10. This is a quote from Nāgārjuna in *Mahā-prajñāpāramitā-upadeśa*
    (T25.1509.184c) with a variation in the final line. (In this text, the
    fourth line of the quatrain is replaced with a line *not* from *Mahā-*

*prajñāpāramitā-upadeśa* and then a non-verse paraphrase of the replaced line.) The *Mahā-prajñāpāramitā-upadeśa* version, as translated in *Nāgārjuna on the Six Perfections*:

You've already shaved your head and donned the dyed robe.
Taking up the clay bowl, you go out on the alms round.
How then can you delight in and be attached to dharmas of frivolity
　　and excitedness?
Since you gain no Dharma benefit, you lose worldly bliss as well.

11. This entire verse is a quote, with very minor variations, from *Mahā-prajñāpāramitā-upadeśa* (T25.1509.184c).

12. *Mahā-prajñāpāramitā-upadeśa* (T25.1509.274c).

13. This entire verse is a quote (with only very minor variations) from *Mahā-prajñāpāramitā-upadeśa* (T25.1509.184c–5a).

14. These two concluding paragraphs are a direct quote from Nāgārjuna's *Mahā-prajñāpāramitā-upadeśa* (T25.1509.185a).

## Chapter Four

1. This corresponds to a quote from the *Sutra on the Ten Grounds* contained in Vasubandhu's treatise devoted to it (十地經論 – T26.1522.169a15).

2. The first "quote" (身安則道隆) is actually a condensing paraphrase of an idea found in multiple locations in the Āgamas and other Indian Buddhist canonical works. (It is not found as a direct quote in a digital search of the extant Indian-origin canon.) In the extant early Chinese-origin canon, it is found as a direct quote only in a Pureland sutra commentary (阿彌陀經義記 – T37.1755.308b) where the phrasing is virtually identical (身安即道隆).

    As for the quatrain, it is found in three closely related editions of the monastic moral code translated by Buddhayaśas, the early sixth-century north Indian translator (四分律比丘戒本 – T22.1429.1022b; 四分僧戒本 – T22.1430.1020a; 四分比丘尼戒本 – T22.1431.1040b).

3. *Sutra on the General Teachings and Remonstrances of the Buddha Prior to Parinirvāṇa*, (佛垂般涅槃略說教誡經 – T12.389.1111a–b).

4. "Slippery" would not be the most apt description in English. This is actually a reference to a circumstance where the respiration has not yet slowed to a point where it is genuinely subtle, but rather flows on in such an unrestrained fashion that one may even hear an audible sound during either inhalation and exhalation. Zhiyi is very explicit about the meaning of this term in another text where he states: "One should regulate the breathing, ensuring that it is neither coarse nor slippery. If during exhalation or inhalation, there is any sound or [the breath] is not fine (i.e. subtle), this is the mark of 'slipperiness.'" (當調息令不澀不滑。若出入有聲及不細即是滑相。[方等三昧行法 – T46.1940.945c]). The difficulty with producing a one-word rendering into English comes from the multiple connotations in Chinese of: "flowing on and on," "being unrestrained," and "being somewhat elusive" to one's attempts to make the respiration adequately subtle for the development of meditative absorption.

5. I've emended the text here to correct what appears to be an obvious scribal error, that of the *Taisho* text reading "two" (二) when it should actually read "three" (三). Not an uncommon occurrence, this only requires the accidental chipping off or light printing of the short middle stroke in the woodblock character for "three."

6. This verse is found nowhere in the *Taisho* version of the Chinese canon aside from other works authored by Zhiyi. In the *Eminent Tiantai Master Zhizhe's Oral Instructions on the Dhyāna Gateway* (天台智者大師禪門口訣 – T46.1919.581a), there is a minor variation in the fourth line and then the addition of a summarizing couplet:

    In moving forward and in stopping, there is a proper sequence.

The coarse and the subtle do not work against each other.
It is just as with the skillful training of a horse.
As with wishing to move on, so it is with wishing to halt.
If one is constantly diligent and careful in this,
One stabilizes the body and mind and then enters dhyāna.

7.  T09.262.41c.

## Chapter Five

1.   This is a quote from *Sutra on the Upāsaka Precepts* (優婆塞戒經 –
     T24.1488.1062b), translated by Dharmarakṣa (385–433 CE).

2.   This is a paraphrastic quote from a Chinese edition of the *Dharmapāda*,
     but with the two statements presented in reverse order     (法句經 –
     T04.210.572a). The precise quote is: "In the absence of dhyāna, one
     does not exercise wisdom. In the absence of wisdom, one does not
     course in dhyāna. The Path comes forth from dhyāna and wisdom."
     (無禪不智。無智不禪。道從禪智。)

# Chapter Six

1. The four types of deportment are walking, standing, sitting, and lying down.

2. I've copied these five bracketed titles from later in the text so as to inform the student ahead of time of the main topics contained in the ensuing eight pages.

3. *Bhikshu Pratimokṣa Precept Manual* (十誦比丘波羅提木叉戒本 – T23.1436.470c).

4. *Sutra on the General Teachings and Remonstrances of the Buddha Prior to Parinirvāṇa* (佛垂般涅槃略說教誡經 – T12.389.1111a).

5. This is the verse spoken by Bhikshu Aśvajit to Śāriputra in explaining the essence of the Buddha's teaching. It is quoted here from the *Middle-Length Sutra on Origination* (中本起經 – T04.196.153c). "Śramaṇa" is a term of reference for a religious mendicant who exerts himself strenuously on a path of spiritual liberation. As such, it is an alternate term of reference for a Buddhist monk. The Bhikshu sums up in this quatrain the nature of the effort by which one might validly be referred to as a "śramaṇa."

6. A *kṣaṇa* is the shortest measure of time. One definition states that sixty of them transpire in a single fingersnap (Soothill, pp. 250–1).

7. 大乘起信論 (T32.1666.582a). There are minor textual variations here from the extant *Taisho* text. The meaning, however, is identical.

8. "True character of dharmas" (諸法實相) is a Sino-Buddhist rendering of the Sanskrit *dharmatā*. It simply refers to dharmas as they truly are. This term points directly to a dharma's "true suchness" (*tathatā*) and absence of any inherent existence. One should not construe from the term that any genuinely independent "reality" is possessed by any particular dharma.

9. *Pratyutpanna Samādhi Sūtra* (般舟三昧經 – T13.418.906a). The entire verse (uttered by the Buddha) is as follows:

   As for the mind, it does not know the mind.
   Possessing mind, one does not perceive the mind.
   If the mind generates thoughts, then this is delusion.
   The absence of thought is nirvāṇa.

   These dharmas are devoid of solidity,
   They are constantly established in one's thoughts.
   Through understanding and perceiving emptiness,
   In every case, one remains free of thinking.

10. "King of Lions" is a metaphoric reference to the Buddha. Master Baojing's commentary notes that when the Buddha lies down, there is no mental dimness, only complete quiescence together with wakeful

awareness (p. 165). This term is also descriptive of a particular posture in which one lies down on the right side with the right arm crooked under the head and with the left arm up on top of the body with the hand on or adjacent to the left hip.

11. This refers to the five concepts discussed earlier, namely, cultivating calming-and-insight as means: 1) to counter the coarseness and dis-orderedness of the beginner's mind; 2) to counter the faults of mental sinking or floating; 3) to accord with whatever is appropriate; 4) to counteract subtle states of mind occurring in meditative absorption; 5) to achieve equal balance in meditative absorption and wisdom.

12. See previous note.

13. *Mahāprajñāpāramitā Sūtra* (摩訶般若波羅蜜經 – T08.223.253b–c).

14. *Mahā-prajñāpāramitā-upadeśa* (T25.1509.161a). There are ten minor vari-ations in the quotation as cited in this text, only one of which involves a noteworthy change of meaning. (The first half of the third stanza therein reads: "When the patch-robed one goes out on the alms round, when moving and stopping, his mind is always one.")

## Chapter Seven

1. "Contemplation of the conventional" and "contemplation of emptiness" are two of the "three contemplations" so central to the Tiantai hermeneutic system. (The third is "contemplation of the middle.")

2. It may be worth noting here that all orthodox Buddhists consider most of the causal factors involved in "roots of goodness" to originate in previous lifetimes. Hence these are not just present-life issues.

3. See Section Eight for a detailed treatment of these issues.

4. *Anāgamya*, often referred to as "access concentration," or "preliminary concentration" is the state of meditative concentration developed just prior to the first dhyāna.

5. Awareness of the entry of the breath, awareness of the exiting of the breath, awareness of the length of the breath, awareness of the breath pervading the body, experiencing joy, experiencing bliss, and mind's generation of bliss are all included within the "sixteen special ascendant practices" (十六特勝). See: Foguang Dictionary, 389a, 482a; Dingfubao Dictionary, 213c; Harivarman's *Satyasiddhi-śāstra* (成實論 – T32.1646.355-6).

6. The nine reflections on impurity (*nava-aśubha-saṃjñā* – 九不淨想]), as explained in *Mahā-prajñāpāramitā-upadeśa* are: 1) the bloated corpse; 2) the bluish corpse; 3) the damaged corpse; 4) the blood-smeared corpse; 5) the purulent, rotting corpse; 6) the corpse which has been gnawed at [by scavenging animals and insects]; 7) the scattered corpse; 8) the skeletal corpse; and 9) the burned corpse (T25.1509.217a-18c).

7. This refers to the eight liberations (*aṣṭau vimokṣāḥ* – 八解脫, also known as: 八背舍).

8. Thus this section refers then not just to compassion but also to all four of the four immeasurable minds (*apramāṇacitta*).

9. This is an abbreviated reference to the entire twelve-fold chain of causation.

10. *Praśrabdhi*, "lightness and easefulness" is one of the wholesome dharmas, is the fourth of the seven limbs of enlightenment, and is a standard feature, common to both mind and body, which arises in beginning meditation states.

11. This is an abbreviated reference to the ten reflections and eight recollections.

12. These are the subcomponents of the thirty-seven wings of enlightenment.

13. This is a reference to the three gates to liberation, otherwise known as the three samādhis.

14. This is probably a reference to the four additional perfections resulting

from the unfolding of the sixth perfection (wisdom) in the formulation known as the ten perfections. The additional four are: skillful means, vows, the powers, and the knowledges.

15. This is from Kumārajīva's translation of the *Sutra on the Buddha's General Instructions and Remonstrances Spoken before Entering Parinirvāṇa* (佛垂般涅槃略說教誡經 – T12.389.1111a).

# Chapter Eight

1.  In his long commentarial work on the *Great Calming-and-Insight* by Master Zhiyi, Zhanran identifies this as a ghost from among the ranks of precept breakers (止觀輔行傳弘決 – T46.1912.409b).

2.  This type of ghost is described in the *Sutra on the Right Dharma Stations of Mindfulness* (正法念處經 – T17.721.92a-b, 100c–101a) translated during the early sixth century by the South Indian monk Prajñāruci. According to that scripture, this "consumer of fire and coals" hungry ghost is number thirty among thirty-six major categories of hungry ghosts. It is a type of hungry ghost which attempts to relieve its perpetual hunger through feasting on various sorts of fire and smoke such as that occurring in funeral pyres.

    Master Baojing identifies the *duiti* ghost as an especially aggravating and fearsome-looking subspecies of *yakṣa* ghost, one which has four eyes and two mouths.

3.  "Name-and-form" is synonymous with the five aggregates which in turn are the bases for our imputing the existence of inherently existing beings of the sorts listed here. "Name" refers to the four aggregates of: feelings (including those arising through not only the five basic sense faculties, but also those arising through the intellectual mind faculty); mental perceptions; karmic formative factors (*saṃskāras*); and the consciousnesses. "Form" is primarily a reference to physical phenomena, including the five sense faculties, the five sense objects, and "forms" perceptible by the intellectual mind faculty.

4.  This is from Buddha's verse to Māra beneath the Bodhi Tree drawn from *Mahā-prajñāpāramitā-upadeśa* (T25.1509.169a). Nāgārjuna provides a fuller version of the same verse in the same work (T25.1509.99b-c) and attributes its origin to the *Kṣudraka-āgama-sūtra* (雜法藏經). Lamotte (p. 341) demonstrates that these verses appear with a few differences in the *Suttanipāta* (see verses 436–449) and the *Lalitavistara*.

5.  "*Vaipulya*" means "expansive." In the broader sense, it is reference to the entire corpus of Great Vehicle sutras. In the narrower sense of the chronological formulation of Tiantai hermeneutics, it refers to the sutras generally spoken after the *Avataṃsaka Sutra* and the *Āgama* scriptures, but before such scriptures as the *Perfection of Wisdom*, the *Lotus*, and the *Nirvāṇa*.

6.  The beginning Dharma student should not be so naive as to think that Master Zhiyi is suggesting any possibility that one would have to sacrifice one's life in the course of exorcising demonic states. The reference is purely to the degree of determination which may be required to accomplish the task in extreme cases, this because enforcing rectitude in one's own thoughts is not always so easy, especially where

one has allowed self-destructive mental habits to become ingrained. It may very well be in such cases that one's determination must be fierce in its level of intensity. In the absence of such strong determination, one may become vulnerable to "lapses."

7.  This is a reference to codes of ethics taken on in formal precept-transmitting ceremonies. Although this usually refers to the monastic's ordination precepts, it may also refer to bodhisattva moral codes available to laity who have already formally taken the five precepts.

8.  This is from *Mahā-prajñāpāramitā-upadeśa* (T25.1509.99b). Nāgārjuna's precise statement there (where he sums up his commentary on the *Mahā-prajñāpāramitā-upadeśa* text's statement: "They have gone beyond all matters associated with demons.") is as follows: "Then again, aside from the true character of dharmas, all other dharmas are entirely [within the sphere of] demons. These include for example all of the afflictions, the fetters, the bondage of desire, the grasping at and becoming entangled in the [five] aggregates, the [eighteen sense] realms, and the [twelve] sense fields, [and includes as well] the demon kings, the demon subjects, and demons in the form of humans."

9.  Also from *Mahā-prajñāpāramitā-upadeśa* (T25.1509.211a), this is drawn from Nāgārjuna's discussion of the four immeasurables wherein the actual quoted lines attributed to the Buddha are slightly variant. I translate here the entire verse:

As for when I sat upon the platform of the Path,
It was such as even wisdom is unable to apprehend.
As with an empty fist employed to trick little children,
It was done in order to bring all to deliverance.

The true character of dharmas
Is identical to the characteristic aspects of beings.
If one seizes upon the characteristic aspects of beings,
Then one strays far away from the path of reality.

If one constantly bears in mind eternally empty characteristics,
Such a person is not engaged in the practice of the Path.
For, among dharmas which are neither produced nor destroyed,
He nonetheless makes discriminations regarding their aspects.

If one makes discriminations and engages in reflective intellection,
This then is just the net of Māra.
If one is unmoving and doesn't depend on anything,
This then constitutes the seal of the Dharma.

# Chapter Nine

1. This is a quote from a discussion of the suffering of sickness drawn from the *Sutra on the Five Kings as Spoken by the Buddha* (佛說五王經 – T14.523.796b). The Buddha so impresses the Kings with his explanation of the eight sufferings that they renounce their palaces and royal pleasures, preferring then to become monks in quest of liberation from cyclic existence.

2. Traditional Chinese medicine employs the term "spleen" to encompass the overall functioning of the digestive system and does not at all limit its use of the term to reference the blood-filtering organ carrying that name in Western medicine.

3. *"Dantian,"* literally translated, means "the field [for cultivating] the pill [of immortality]." The binome is a Chinese anatomical term with origins in Taoist yoga. The term was adopted into Buddhist literature as the nearest indigenous analogue to the identically located *maṇipūra* chakra of such importance in Indian Buddhist meditation yoga.

4. T14.475.545a.

5. Master Baojing cautions the reader to not rely on the actual meaning of the character so much as on intoning the sound of the character while exhaling very subtly and performing the related visualization (250-1).

6. I'm emending the Taisho text here, substituting "two" (二) for "one" (一) to correct an obvious scribal error. The emendation is supported by other editions as well as by the flow of ideas contained in the text.

## Chapter Ten

1.  It may be useful to reflect that Zhiyi is not criticizing this level of realization *per se*, but rather is pointing out that developing a non-progressing attachment to it is fatal to pursuit of the bodhisattva's career which eventually culminates in buddhahood.

2.  From a verse uttered by Mahākāśyapa in the "Faith and Understanding" chapter of the *Lotus Sutra* (妙法蓮華經 – T09.262.18b).

3.  A term indicating a station synonymous with the path of seeing constituting a "point of no return" for those intent on the individual-liberation goal of arhatship.

4.  This means "right enlightenment" and refers here to the enlightenment of a buddha.

5.  From the *Bodhisattva Necklace Sutra* (菩薩瓔珞本業經 – T24.1485.1014b, c). The post-ellipsis quote is located a full *Taisho* panel after the first quote.

6.  Master Baojing points out that the two types of emptiness refer here to the emptiness of persons and the emptiness of dharmas (281).

7.  *Sarvajñatā* is the omniscience or all-knowledge of a buddha.

8.  From Nāgārjuna's *Treatise on the Middle* (中論 – T30.1564.33b).

9.  This is a quote from "The Analogies Chapter" of the *Lotus Sutra* where the great white ox which represents the one buddha vehicle is being described (T9.262.12c). Master Baojing notes that "even and correct" refers to the equality of meditative absorption and wisdom characteristic of a buddha's perfect contemplation whereas "speed as fleet as the wind" refers to that perfect contemplation's acuity in reflecting the nature and its entry into the way of effortlessness (290-1).

10. Again, this is from the *Bodhisattva Necklace Sutra* (菩薩瓔珞本業經 – T24.1485.1014c).

11. *Lotus Sutra* (T09.262.30c). This is a slight paraphrase. The actual passage states, "One carries on the endeavors of the Tathāgata."

12. *Ibid.* (T09.262.31c). Master Baojing notes that in this additional quote from the *Lotus Sutra*, the "practice" refers to the practice of a buddha wherein a single practice embodies all practices, the "robe" refers to patience, the "room" refers to the great loving-kindness and compassion, and the "seat" refers to the emptiness of dharmas (291-2).

13. Master Baojing also notes that "adornment" here refers to the merit and wisdom of a buddha (292).

14. From the *Avataṃsaka Sutra* (大方廣佛華嚴經 – T09.278.449c).

15. Ibid. T09.278.452c.

16. Ibid. T09.278.452c.

17. From the *Mahāparinirvāṇa Sutra* (大般涅槃經 – T12.374.590a).

18. From the *Lotus Sutra* (妙法蓮華經 – T09.262.19c). The text I have sup-
    plied in brackets represents a more complete quotation from the sutra
    text.

19. The three qualities alluded to are: prajñā, liberation, and the Dharma
    body.

20. From the composite edition of the *Golden Light Sutra* (合部金光明經 –
    T16.664.362b-c). The bracketed phrases reflect the fuller phrasing of
    the scripture text as currently recorded in *Taisho*. The extant *Taisho*
    edition has the order of the last two statements reversed and so con-
    cludes with: "The Tathāgatas during the intermediate phase engage
    in all sorts of adornments of the Dharma realm of beings and in every
    case it is for the sake of benefiting others."

21. From the *Pratyutpanna Samādhi Sutra* (般舟三昧經 – T13.418.909a). The
    extant *Taisho* edition reads slightly differently:

    "It is from the mind that all Buddhas understand and realize the Path.
    As for the mind, it is pure, bright, and undefiled.
    In the five destinies, it is fresh and immaculate and takes on no form.
    Where there is one who understands this, he perfects the great Path."

22. The three obstacles are those associated with afflictions, with karma,
    and with karmic retribution.

23. As articulated in the extensive discussion earlier in this work, the five
    hindrances are: desire, ill-will, lethargy-and-sleepiness, excitedness-
    and-regretfulness, doubt.

SOURCE TEXT VARIANT READINGS

[0462001] 【原】萬曆十年刊增上寺報恩藏本，【甲】德川時代刊宗教大學藏本

[0462002] （偈云）＋諸【甲】

[0470001] 〔矣〕－【甲】

[0472001] 一＝二【甲】

正
體
字

[0462001] 【原】万历十年刊增上寺报恩藏本，【甲】德川时代刊宗教大学藏本

[0462002] （偈云）＋诸【甲】

[0470001] 〔矣〕－【甲】

[0472001] 一＝二【甲】

简
体
字

## About the Translator

Bhikshu Dharmamitra (ordination name "Heng Shou" – 釋恆授) is a Chinese-tradition translator-monk and one of the early American disciples (since 1968) of the late Weiyang Ch'an patriarch, Dharma teacher, and exegete, the Venerable Master Hsuan Hua (宣化上人). He has a total of 23 years in robes during two periods as a monastic (1969–1975; 1991 to present).

Dharmamitra's principle educational foundations as a translator lie in four years of intensive monastic training and Chinese-language study of classic Mahāyāna texts in a small-group setting under Master Hua from 1968–1972, undergraduate Chinese language study at Portland State University, a year of intensive one-on-one Classical Chinese study at the Fu Jen University Language Center near Taipei, and two years at the University of Washington's School of Asian Languages and Literature (1988–90).

Since taking robes again under Master Hua in 1991, Dharmamitra has devoted his energies primarily to study and translation of classic Mahāyāna texts with a special interest in works by Ārya Nāgārjuna and related authors. To date, he has translated a dozen important texts, most of which are slated for publication by Kalavinka Press.

# Kalavinka Buddhist Classics Title List

## Meditation Instruction Texts

### The Essentials of Buddhist Meditation
A marvelously complete classic *śamathā-vipaśyanā* (calming-and-insight) meditation manual. By Tiantai Śramaṇa Zhiyi (538–597 CE).

### The Six Gates to the Sublime
The earliest Indian Buddhist meditation method explaining the essentials of breath and calming-and-insight meditation. By Śramaṇa Zhiyi.

## Bodhisattva Path Texts

### Nāgārjuna on the Six Perfections
Chapters 17–30 of Ārya Nāgārjuna's *Mahāprājñāpāramitā Upadeśa*.

### Marvelous Stories from the Perfection of Wisdom
130 stories from Ārya Nāgārjuna's *Mahāprājñāpāramitā Upadeśa*.

### A Strand of Dharma Jewels (Ārya Nāgārjuna's *Ratnāvalī*)
The earliest extant edition, translated by Paramārtha: *ca* 550 CE

### Nāgārjuna's Guide to the Bodhisattva Path
The *Bodhisaṃbhāra Treatise* with abridged Vaśitva commentary.

### The Bodhisaṃbhāra Treatise Commentary
The complete exegesis by the Indian Bhikshu Vaśitva (*ca* 300–500 CE).

### Letter from a Friend - The Three Earliest Editions
The earliest extant editions of Ārya Nāgārjuna's *Suhṛlekkha*:

| | |
|---|---|
| Translated by Tripiṭaka Master Guṇavarman | (*ca* 425 CE) |
| Translated by Tripiṭaka Master Saṅghavarman | (*ca* 450 CE) |
| Translated by Tripiṭaka Master Yijing | (*ca* 675 CE) |

## Resolve-for-Enlightenment Texts

### On Generating the Resolve to Become a Buddha
*On the Resolve to Become a Buddha* by Ārya Nāgārjuna
*Exhortation to Resolve on Buddhahood* by Patriarch Sheng'an Shixian
*Exhortation to Resolve on Buddhahood* by the Tang Literatus, Peixiu

### Vasubandhu's Treatise on the Bodhisattva Vow
By Vasubandhu Bodhisattva (*ca* 300 CE)

*All Kalavinka Press translations include facing-page source text.

CPSIA information can be obtained
at www.ICGtesting.com
Printed in the USA
BVOW08s0210160218

508098BV00002B/152/P